THE
ARGUMENT
HANGOVER

THE
ARGUMENT
HANGOVER

EMPOWERING COUPLES TO
FIGHT SMARTER AND OVERCOME
COMMUNICATION PITFALLS

JOCELYN & AARON
"THE FREEMANS"

Skyhorse Publishing

Skyhorse Publishing books may be purchased in bulk at special discounts
for sales promotion, corporate gifts, fund-raising, or educational
purposes. Special editions can also be created to specifications. For
details, contact the Special Sales Department, Skyhorse Publishing,
307 West 36th Street, 11th Floor, New York, NY 10018 or
info@skyhorsepublishing.com.

Skyhorse® and Skyhorse Publishing® are registered trademarks of
Skyhorse Publishing, Inc.®, a Delaware corporation.

Visit our website at www.skyhorsepublishing.com.

10 9 8 7 6 5 4 3

Library of Congress Cataloging-in-Publication Data is available on file.

Cover design by Daniel Brount
Cover illustration by Shutterstock

Print ISBN: 978-1-5107-6341-8
Ebook ISBN: 978-1-5107-6342-5

Printed in China

An Invitation to My Partner and Teammate, _____.

I invite you to read this book with me and to have fun along the way as we grow. Our relationship is the key to our lives thriving and our dreams being fulfilled. I desire to strengthen our relationship and to learn more about how we can be even better partners for each other and design a life we love together as a team.

This book is my gift for both of us as an expression of how much our relationship means to me.

Will you read this with me?

[ ] Yes.

[ ] Absolutely!

[ ] I'm already on chapter two!

With love and gratitude, _____

TABLE OF CONTENTS

ABOUT THE AUTHORS

Hey, we're the Freemans! Before you dive into this book, we wanted to introduce ourselves a little more. Our relationship didn't start off like your favorite romance movie, and it certainly wasn't rainbows and butterflies of bliss. In fact, I (Aaron) tried to break up with Jocelyn within the first six months of our relationship.

You see, up until I was twenty-eight, I had convinced myself that relationships weren't for me. Though I might have said "I don't need one," it was really because of past dating experiences of being broken up with and hurt over and over that I started keeping myself at a safe distance when it came to relationships. So here I was just a few months into dating Jocelyn and I called her on a hot summer day and said "I think we should just be friends." This was to her surprise and probably shock because things were going great in our relationship. But this was coming from a deep subconscious fear that it was only a matter of time before this would end, so I better do it first. She called me back just three minutes later and said "that doesn't work for me." In that moment, I knew that she wasn't going to be someone that easily gave up in the tough moments. It was really powerful and healing for me, so I said "Okay, I'm in. Let's do this!"

Here's the thing, that moment didn't make up for the fact that we had completely different upbringings and different views of relationships from what we observed from our parents. To be blunt, we weren't on the same page about how to communicate and handle conflict. Aaron picked up patterns of avoiding conflict and holding back more vulnerable feelings, and I (Jocelyn) picked up habits of taking out my emotion and fighting in destructive ways. This led us down a path of discovering and learning all the skills and tools we didn't learn growing up to really set ourselves up for a lasting relationship.

You see, we don't believe love is enough to guarantee that a relationship will last, or that it will thrive and be fulfilling as the years go on. After mastering the relationship skills in our own relationship, we had couples ask us left and right "what is it that you're doing to be as connected as you are?" We quickly realized that our society mostly focuses on relationships in two ways: finding the partner and getting married, then resorting to counseling when in crisis. We thought *what about something in between? What about learning relationship skills without it meaning something is wrong?* Just like you would do ongoing education or training to get better at a sport, physical health, or your career.

These questions led us to create Empowered Couples University, which hosts both online and in-person workshops, courses, and coaching for modern couples. We have written two books, personally coached hundreds of couples, led over 42 events for couples and hundreds of online courses, and also created a highly sought after and accredited relationship coaching certification to train other aspiring coaches.

We're beyond grateful that our teachings have reached over a million couples, and we're not stopping anytime soon. This is our life purpose, and we're so excited to empower your relationship. Diving into this book is a great place to start.

Website: www.MeetTheFreemans.com
Instagram: @Meet_TheFreemans
Facebook: @Meetthefreemansauthors
Podcast: The Empowered Couples Podcast

INTRODUCTION

Hey, new friend! We're the Freemans and we encourage you to ask yourself these questions before reading further. You see, there's a difference between reading a book and saying "that's a nice idea, I liked that book" and actually using and leveraging a book to impact your daily life (more so actually implementing the tools into your relationship). These questions will help you do that.

1. Am I open to implementing new habits and beliefs to make my relationship be even better?
You've probably heard the quote, "Insanity is doing the same thing over and over again and expecting a different result." But if you're honest with yourself, do you try the same things repeatedly in your relationship and wonder why things haven't changed? This book is an invitation for you to not just pick up new ideas, but to truly implement new habits and skills for your relationship. At first it might be uncomfortable, but over time you will have a relationship with an even stronger connection and fantastic communication, which will stand the test of time.

2. Am I willing to let go of "being right" about my relationship?
"But I am right!" How often do we think that or say that out loud? Truthfully, all human beings have a subconscious desire (even *need*) to be right. You might have started to put your relationship into a certain box, like "they're not a good listener" or "we're never going to improve" or, even worse, "they're the one that needs to change!"

But would you rather be right about your perspective, or open to growth? As you journey into this book, can you commit to being more concerned about understanding each other than arguing about why you have the right perspective?

3. Am I open to even more love and connection in my relationship?

This question might seem unnecessary because you're thinking, *well, of course I want more love and connection.* But what you might not realize is that sometimes you think things are as good as they can get, or that you're just past the "honeymoon" phase and peak of passion and excitement of the relationship. Perhaps you even wonder if you're worthy enough for the most outrageously incredible, miraculous, love-filled relationship. Is there really more that you can let in?

4. Am I willing to play 100 percent in my relationship (unconditionally)?

It's tempting to only put in as much effort and energy into the relationship that we see our partner putting in. In fact, most people start a relationship putting in 100 percent effort, but then slowly let themselves coast down to 75 percent, then 50 percent, or even 25 percent. An incredible relationship doesn't happen by accident, and it doesn't stay that way without intention and practice. Throughout your relationship there will be times when you feel you are putting in more effort, and other times when your partner is. But this question is here to ask you if you are willing to play *full out* in your partnership to grow stronger than ever (no matter what circumstances and challenges come up). A truly empowered couple sees their relationship as 100/100, not 50/50.

Okay, now that you're committed to being open to new ideas, beliefs, and habits throughout this journey, we can dive in deeper. And you'll soon find out that this book is designed as a practical tool for you to use with your partner.

1

WHAT IS THE ARGUMENT HANGOVER?

"Peace is not the absence of conflict, but the ability to cope with it."

—Mahatma Gandhi

You've had a hangover, right? Well, depending on your lifestyle, the two most common hangover types are: the "food hangover" and the "alcohol hangover." We'd like to start this book off with a funny story about the best example of a food hangover that we experienced. (Don't worry, you didn't pick up a cookbook—we'll explain how this relates to your relationship soon.)

What time of year comes to mind when you think of a food hangover? It was, of course, Thanksgiving! If you are also thinking, *well, here comes a story about Aaron eating too much* . . . sorry, you're wrong. This is actually a story about Jocelyn as soon as she saw the desserts come out on the table after the Thanksgiving meal. Now, this might not sound surprising to you at all if you can imagine your own Thanksgiving (you may even know the experience all too well)!

When we gathered with Jocelyn's family on this particular Thanksgiving feast a few years ago, there was so much food. Imagine a huge open kitchen layout in the modern farmhouse style home, two ovens running on full blast for hours, and a 10-foot island that

1

was just waiting to be filled with all the food going in and out of those two workhorse ovens. By the time the twelve of us were ready to eat, we looked at the spread in front of us as if we were waiting to feed the entire New England Patriots' offensive line. The food seemed endless.

Once we got through the main course of traditional turkey, potatoes, stuffing, cranberry sauce, and Brussels sprouts (oh, and if that last one surprised you, it was just as much of a surprise to Aaron to see Brussels as a Thanksgiving staple since he grew up in Ohio), we took a break to relax and gather ourselves for the next wave that was to come . . . the desserts.

This is the part that was so funny to watch and eventually led to Jocelyn experiencing a food hangover like never before. Jocelyn typically has a very specific, routine, and healthy lifestyle when it comes to food, so from Aaron's perspective it was quite a wonderful joy to see her just "let herself go" to enjoy all the desserts. For our family, one of the key dessert items is pecan pie, so there were at least two pecan pies among pumpkin pies, pumpkin cupcakes, brownies, and ice cream. Jocelyn's eyes got huge as the 10-foot island now displayed the scene of a homestyle bakery. This was an opportunity for her to really indulge in all these treats and desserts that she doesn't usually enjoy, so she went off after three pumpkin cupcakes, multiple pieces of pumpkin pie with whipped cream swirled on top, and the main staple, Grandma's famous pecan pie. (Imagine the pecan pie just coming out of the oven, warm and gooey while somehow crisp all at the same time.) She was certainly enjoying herself and let us all know with the remarks she was making while eating. This (at the time, of course) seemed like the best idea ever to her!

Just a few hours later, she was in the first phases of the food hangover. At first her stomach felt so full and stretched to its limits that it began to hurt. She felt jittery and even a little light-headed. She soon asked Aaron to drive home because her body and muscles were shaking. On the ride home it was hard for her to process thoughts in her mind let alone speak out loud in clear and coherent sentences. By the time we got home it was difficult for her to sleep because her body was restless. In this case, the amount of sugar she consumed was a shock to her system. Needless to say, she didn't sleep well that night.

The next morning, Jocelyn's energy was low, her body felt weak, and she didn't have enthusiasm to do much of anything besides lay on the couch, regretful of the "actions" she took the previous evening. Does any of this sound familiar to the hangovers that you have had? What once seemed like a good idea, which in the moment did actually feel good, had now produced the totally opposite effect, leaving her wishing that she could even take some of it back! (Don't tell us that you have never thought, *I am* never *doing that again* . . .)

This is the example of a "food hangover," but we bet you are already starting to understand how this relates to what we call "the Argument Hangover." Whether it's food, alcohol, or an argument, a hangover is the result of something being overdone. Yes, it may have felt like the right thing to do in the moment, yet the next day you feel sorry and regretful for the actions you took; this leaves you feeling lethargic, tired, run-down, or even sick.

Now, what does this have to do with your relationship and your experience of an Argument Hangover? Well, isn't this exactly how you feel after you have had an emotionally heated argument with your partner? Oxford Languages defines an argument as an exchange of diverging or opposite views, typically a heated or angry one. The Argument Hangover is what comes after a disagreement with your partner that triggered high emotion. This surge of emotion can leave you feeling:

- Tired and run-down because it took so much out of you
- Angry or resentful for what was said and done
- Tense in your neck and shoulders

- Regretful for what you said and how you said it
- Unsure of how/when to reconnect
- Pain in your vocal cords if you got to the point of yelling
- Apathy and resignation if not addressed soon

> The Argument Hangover is the period of time between having an argument with your partner and fully resolving it *emotionally* to reconnect as a couple.

| the original argument | the argument hangover | fully resolved + reconnected |

The length of time you experience these emotions can vary widely. The Argument Hangover can last anywhere from five minutes to three days or more. For some couples we work with, they've had a subtle lingering Argument Hangover for two or three years that they just got used to tolerating, like a sore neck that became normal. Other couples might think *oh, we are good because we don't fight often or ever.* But that could be a symptom of suppressing thoughts or feelings from each other and avoiding challenging subjects. If you're in that place, this book will greatly benefit you, so you can bring up tough subjects without emotions getting escalated or feeling defeated.

Many things might happen during an Argument Hangover that can leave you feeling disconnected from your partner or carrying emotional residue from the exchange. You might think back and wonder *why did I raise my voice? Why did I say that? Why did I swear? I really wish I hadn't done that. I wish I could go back and take back those actions.* If you stay in the Argument Hangover as you head to sleep that evening, you might not sleep well because you haven't come back to connection. You may find yourself replaying the things they said over and over again, and wondering if they really meant what they said or if their words were only said in the heat of the moment. You feel hurt and disappointed, and after you reflect on it, you probably ask yourself the same questions, thinking *why did I say that thing about their parents again? I know that I should never compare her to her mother . . . but I did it anyway.*

So here you are, feeling very similar to a hangover from food or alcohol, yet it's actually the result of an argument. The fundamental question to ask yourself is how long is this feeling going to last? Five minutes? Half of a day? Weeks? It could be something that happens frequently, so you're tired and wonder *is this us? Is it the relationship? Is there anything we can even do?* Or things could seem fine and all of a sudden you have these big blowups that seems to come out of nowhere. Well, these blowups are actually the remnants of past Argument Hangovers that never got fully resolved. This is the biggest difference between the food and alcohol type of hangovers. Just imagine one of your past hangovers for a moment. Thankfully you felt better after a couple of days of rest and letting your body detox. But what if it lasted for a few weeks? What if, just when you thought you were recovered, a month later all of a sudden like a car crash you got hit again with the same feeling? What if this periodically happened for years?

This is what is happening for many people when it comes to the Argument Hangover because they are not actually resolving the emotional impact of the argument. The bottom line is that most people don't actually know how to handle this period of time and are not yet equipped with the skills needed to get themselves through an Argument Hangover properly so that it doesn't continue to have a negative impact on their relationship.

It isn't you or your partner's fault. We were never taught how to fight smarter. Did you have a Relationships 101 class in school? No, none of us did. You can feel relief knowing you are not alone and this is the norm right now. We reviewed data from a group of 78 couples who took the number-one relationship P/E assessment in the world today (it's been taken by four million couples over the last 40 years).[1] These couples ranged in age from 25 to 64, from engaged to married 32 years, with household incomes between $50,000 and $225,000+, various faiths, races, and cultures, and including couples with no kids, and parents with young kids and adult children. The average score from these couples shows their communication satisfaction was a 36.67 (out of 100) and their conflict resolution satisfaction was a 36.41 (out of 100). As you can see, the majority of couples can objectively use some assistance with these two critical areas of their relationship. We will refer to more of these assessment results throughout the book.

We share those results to show you that you are not alone in the relationship challenges you face. We've had the privilege of sharing relationship principles with over one million people and watching couples implement the skills offered in this book to experience a complete 180-degree turn in their relationship. We've worked with couples on the brink of divorce because their fights were so toxic and hurtful, couples who have experienced infidelity leading to broken trust, couples with massive disagreements about how to parent and define their relationship roles, and so many other challenging circumstances.

For each of these couples, it initially felt like what they were going through wasn't going to ever get better. But by implementing the right relationship skills, they now say things like:

> "Our family is inspired to work harder on their own relationships because of our example."

---

1 Prepare/Enrich. "The Assessment." https://www.prepare-enrich.com/ (accessed January 2018).

- "We've rebuilt our trust to be stronger than before."
- "We finally understand each other's perspectives, and have come up with parenting strategies that we both believe in."

How did they achieve these triumphs? They made a powerful decision and decided to commit themselves to learning and practicing the tools and skills we teach in this book.

We have heard it all, and we promise you, you're not alone in what you're experiencing. You also don't have to feel like anything is "wrong" or "bad" in your relationship to massively benefit from this book. You can be in a happy, loving relationship and still become even better communicators and have your disagreements become areas that make your relationship stronger. In fact, we've worked with couples who feel very successful in all areas of their lives, but still admit that communication and conflict resolution with their partner could use some improvement. This challenge happens for couples from all walks of life! We've even worked with celebrities and affluent corporate executives who are very talented, but are not skilled in these areas. We went to Thailand and talked to a local merchant there who expressed almost verbatim the same communication challenges as these celebrity couples. So, wherever you live, whatever you do for a living, you aren't alone in wanting to learn to "fight smarter."

THE GOAL OF THE ARGUMENT HANGOVER

Here's the thing, the goal is not to avoid arguments and keep conflicts from coming up. That's not what a relationship and a marriage is really about! In fact, it's totally unrealistic to even try and live without challenges. Like we said a minute ago, it could be an indication that you're too comfortable or not talking about deeper needs and wants that can feel challenging to bring up (we'll talk about avoiding conflict later on).

You and your partner are different people, with different life experiences that have shaped the way you see the world. Of course,

7

you see situations differently (even if slightly) than all of the other eight billion people on the planet, so you should not expect to get into a relationship and have your partner see things exactly the same way as you do. It can be tough to accept, but their reality is their reality and it's valid. Just like your reality is also valid.

Seeing things differently from one another is a great thing! Just like companies, cultures, and countries experience progress through having their ideas and norms challenged, acknowledging your partner's beliefs will keep your relationship strong. If you always agreed, you would both be stagnant, not growing or evolving, which can feel mundane. You don't want to be married or in a relationship with yourself anyway, right? That would be really boring! You got together with your partner for a lot of the reasons that make them unique, but you may try so hard to get them to see things the same way you do, to make you happy, and to fulfill your needs, that you forget you're also here to understand their needs and together work toward a mutually fulfilling relationship.

If you're now accepting that you will in fact have different perspectives, why would you still avoid conflicts? Sure, you don't *love* the feeling of being disagreed with (we'll talk about that later), but the real reason you avoid them is because of the impact of the Argument Hangover on both you and your partner.

The way you fight and the length of your Argument Hangover is what hurts the relationship. More specifically it's what happens (or doesn't happen) during the disagreement and the hangover that cause even more pain than the initial disagreement. The Gottman Institute, which has sought to study and discover what makes a marriage really work and how to predict whether a marriage will end in divorce, asserts that it's how you interact with your partner that leads to relationship success or "failure."[2] It's when you begin to

---

2   Gottman, John M. *The Seven Principles For Making Marriage Work.* New York: Three Rivers Press, 1999.

interact with your partner from a place of defensiveness, criticism, resentment, or shutting them out that puts you on the path of significantly damaging the relationship. These are the biggest signals to look for during an Argument Hangover, as well as how fast your conflicts escalate. When you are in a fight with your partner, does it quickly turn to blame and criticism and re-trigger hurts from the past, or does it start up slowly but lead to you both giving up and shutting down because it doesn't go anywhere? The longer and more frequently the Argument Hangover occurs, the more you will start to feel resentment toward your partner.

The real goal in the beginning is for the Argument Hangover period to become shorter and shorter. If you've been experiencing Argument Hangovers that last for days or weeks, imagine what it would be like to have this last only a few hours. What if it was even a few minutes? From there, what if it didn't escalate to the level of regret, feeling sorry for the things that you said that hurt your partner, and causing rifts in your personal connection?

Remember, this is not about seeing things the same way and always agreeing! This is about the way in which you handle conflict as a couple. It's about the way in which you handle differences of opinion so that you don't react with so much unconscious emotion.

Your focus can be on managing your emotions so they don't escalate so far that you fall into these triggered patterns of saying things you didn't mean, leaving the house, or threatening the relationship, all causing more damage than the initial topic of the argument in the first place. That's one of the things that the Argument Hangover does. How often did a disagreement start as something really small and then sometime later you regret the things you said, you feel disconnected from your partner, and you wonder *how did we even get here*? Or *How did this even start in the first place*?

WHAT DO YOU REALLY WANT FOR YOUR RELATIONSHIP?

This book seeks to help you and your partner shorten the Argument Hangover period and get back on the same team quickly, even if you disagree. We aim to help you remember that you are in a partnership and that you can even be grateful for the ways in which your partner sees things differently. Before every Argument Hangover, you know that all you really wanted was for your partner to hear and understand you. You want to feel like you're on the same team! You want to feel like you're moving the relationship forward and progressing together.

We are going to get a little deep here for a minute but this is really what you came for.

The real purpose of life (next to just living) is to evolve and become the best version of yourself. You want to understand and realize just who you came to be while living on this Earth for a short period of time. Referring to the best definition of success from Earl Nightingale: "Success is the progressive realization of a worthy ideal." What could be more worthy than becoming and expressing the fullest potential of who you really are?

That said, there is no better feeling of success than being in a relationship that can accelerate and magnify your self-development. What could be better than also realizing this ideal alongside another person who wants to go on that journey with you? Does this happen for two people by avoiding conflict or by trying to change that person to better serve you? No! Your focus in reading this book is to implement these conflict resolution tools yourself, and to empower your partner to do the same.

Allow the challenges to come, embrace the times you see things differently, make your Argument Hangover periods shorter and shorter, and leverage them to get back on the right path and become who you were always meant to be together!

As we type that statement, we know it's not an easy undertaking from our own personal experience. We individually and together had many destructive patterns to break that were formed from our vastly different upbringings and some of our formative romantic relationships. You see, Aaron came from a family that was very loving and his parents never fought in front of him, so he didn't see an example of how both partners share their emotions and work through it. Whereas I (Jocelyn) witnessed my parents' very tumultuous divorce. As you read these examples, you might even start to reflect on your own upbringing and how it compares to your partner's. It's important to recognize it because it *does* influence how you communicate and approach conflict, and we'll address that at different times throughout the book. As Aaron and I continued our self-development journey, we realized how each of our romantic relationships influenced us as well, which were again very different. I started to repeat a lot of the destructive patterns I saw growing up—yelling, name calling, and blaming. Aaron was instead withholding his emotions and not talking about how he felt with anyone he dated. These differences of course led to conflicting ideas about how to handle a disagreement.

You see, it wasn't a fairy tale beginning for our relationship. In fact, Aaron tried to break up with me within the first two and a half months of dating. It was an unexpected call to receive on an average, hot day in Arizona. The moment he said, "This is getting too serious for me, I think we should just be friends," my jaw dropped from feeling blindsided. Things seemed great before that moment, so I needed a moment to process it and we hung up for a few minutes. I thought about my two options: One, I could play the game of, "If he wants me, he'll make it happen," or, "I shouldn't have to fight for him." The second option was to put my heart on the line and take a stand for the relationship. I didn't want to wonder *what if* . . . because I was afraid of being vulnerable. I only considered the second option because I knew that he wasn't trying to end it because he didn't enjoy the relationship, but because fear was coming up for him. He had been hurt in the past and had not really worked through it, so he feared it would happen again and followed his tendency of retracting and not sharing his true feelings.

I felt sick to my stomach but called him back and immediately said "That doesn't work for me." Long story short, my statement showed him that I wasn't going to give up easily and I'd stick with him through the uncomfortable moments. You're likely dying to hear his response, which was, "I'm back in!" And he really was fully in.

We both played full-out in learning and mastering the skills for having a healthy, strong relationship. We didn't want to repeat either of our past experiences, so we committed to the "work" individually and together. Which is why we wrote this book for you. To make it an enjoyable (not without it's challenging moments) experience to confront your fears, tendencies, and take a stand for your relationship!

Reading this book is your stand for yourself, your partner, and your relationship, and we are so excited to be on this journey with you. Our hope is that you get the sense that we aren't writing from a "we are perfect and have it all figured out" place, but instead a "we are in this work with you," and the only way we've been able to teach it is by encountering it over and over again too.

As you dive into this journey, you will first uncover a new way to look at conflict and how it can actually support you two in becoming stronger together. You will then identify any unconscious cultural beliefs and "norms" that have contributed to how you might avoid conflict, followed by what internal emotional triggers you have that may instigate recurring disagreements. Then, we'll distinguish the different stages of conflict: before, during, and after; and what you can do in each stage to fight smarter as a couple. Last but not least, you'll enjoy discovering that you actually have a "communication personality type" as a way you can understand how to best communicate with each other about important matters. Learn how to fight smarter and shorten the Argument Hangover by reading the rest of this book (not just letting it gather dust on your bedside table)!

2
OUTDATED BELIEFS ABOUT CONFLICT

"Knowing others is intelligence; knowing yourself is true wisdom. Mastering others is strength; mastering yourself is true power."

—Lao Tzu

After you read that first chapter, you're hopefully feeling encouraged and excited, thinking *tell me the actions to take to shorten the Argument Hangover*! But we have to pause here because this is a common pitfall that many couples fall into when they want to make changes in their relationship. You might read relationship books, watch videos online, or even attend counseling to find the next *action* to take. You could become so fixated on learning the new action that your results do not pan out the way you hoped. Why is that?

For the new actions to stick, you have to change what you believe about conflict or maybe even what you believe about relationships as a whole. Your beliefs unconsciously drive the actions you take, but you don't have to take our word for it. Dozens of leaders and teachers have been speaking about the power of your beliefs throughout history: from Jesus and Buddha to self-development leaders like Tony Robbins, Jim Rohn, and the list goes on. Earl Nightingale poignantly said, "These things we bring on ourselves through our habitual way of thinking." Like us, you likely weren't taught this in grade school. Yes, your results in life come from your actions, but it's your beliefs that drive the actions you take. This is especially true in your relationship, which is why you can react in ways that you feel like you didn't consciously choose. They're just automatic for you, unless you decide to consciously change your beliefs about your relationship and partner first.

We won't go too deep into this because you're likely thinking *we're ready to get started*, but it's important to at least acknowledge that many of the underlying causes of unease (and a gnarly Argument Hangover) in your relationship stem from outdated/unhealthy beliefs about what a relationship should be like. Some of these beliefs are ingrained in you from your culture, your local community, your upbringing, or your formative romantic relationships. Even movies and television shows that you've watched have influenced the way you see relationships and conflict, much of which is not realistic or healthy. Most of the lessons and beliefs are pure junk, to be honest. That's why we'll take you through some of the most common destructive beliefs before we move into the actions you can start to take. Here are some outdated/unhealthy beliefs that will not serve your relationship moving forward:

THE "PICK YOUR BATTLES" BELIEF

We were at a client's wedding that Aaron was asked to officiate (we are both ordained to lead ceremonies). An hour before the wedding, the bride asked her friends, her mom, and other siblings to share their final piece of "relationship wisdom" so she could take it into their first year of marriage. The first person said "remember to keep dating each other," which is always a great reminder. The second person, who happened to be the mother of the bride, said what we consider to be some of the worst relationship advice ever: "Honey, pick your battles." We honestly mean no offense when we say this is horrible advice, and we know this loving mother just wanted her daughter to have a successful marriage. As a relationship coach, it was a tiny bit hard for Jocelyn not to correct her, so she just smiled and said cheers with everyone's champagne flutes in hand. (Don't worry, we had already taken that couple through preparing for marriage coaching, so they knew to take that advice with a grain of salt.)

After the ceremony, I shared this mother's "wisdom" with Aaron because, well, we obviously love to talk about all things relationships. We discussed for a moment before heading out on the dance floor, how millions of couples receive that advice from someone in their life and it sets them up for unhealthy conflict beliefs and patterns later on. Here's why . . .

The entire premise behind the saying "pick your battles" is based on one or more of the following false beliefs about conflict:

- Conflict is bad and should be avoided.
- You aren't going to like your partner's reaction.
- It's not completely "safe" to share all your emotions, thoughts, fears, and needs.
- Your partner will get "fed up" if you bring up the same topics over and over.
- It's better to "walk on eggshells" than to upset your partner.
- There is one "winner" and one "loser" in disagreements.

These beliefs are either inherited from someone else and then keep getting passed down from one generation to the next, or are formed from having repetitive negative relationship experiences in your own life. Just because something has been done one way, for however long it may be, does not mean it is the most constructive or best way to continue. George from our community described this in his own experience by saying, **"I avoid conflict and stuff down my feel-ings, and my spouse will hold on to resentment for days, weeks, or months. I am seen as the problem for her, so then I shut down and** don't follow through due to the hurt of always being the problem and not just part of the problem." So many people have had similar negative experiences around conflict, that many, like George, start to "pick their battles" instead of learning how to fight smarter. (As a side note, this "pick your battles" advice is actually a cousin to another common saying: "don't rock the boat." Which, by the way, is the next worst piece of advice you can give.)

Look, if you're interested in a marriage or committed relationship where you just avoid conflicts to keep from upsetting your partner for fear of losing the relationship, don't take our advice. You can actually stop reading this book now because it's not going to be for you. But if you want to actually deepen your connection, grow as an individual, and as a couple, then you will need to shift the way you see conflict and learn healthy skills.

It's important for you to understand that "picking your battles" is such bad advice for the toxic effect it can have over the years.

> Avoiding conflict in the short-term builds resentment in the long-term.

Think of it like this: imagine that you're wearing a backpack around in life, and every time you avoid a conflict and withhold the thoughts and emotions that are important to you, it adds a two-pound brick to your backpack. The first brick on your back would barely be noticeable, and adding another two pounds wouldn't even be a big deal. But as you continue to add them on, one by one, year after year, wearing that backpack starts to wear down your energy and strength. That same feeling happens in your relationship when you "pick your battles." Instead of adding two pounds of weight to your backpack, you are building up feelings of being suppressed, not understood, and taken for granted. Maybe you can carry this burden for a while but it is guaranteed to diminish the connection and love you have with your partner until you buckle under the weight of resentment toward them and the relationship. So, do yourself and your relationship a favor and keep the bricks from being added to your backpack by not avoiding the conflicts and "picking your battles." If you are reading this right now and feel like you already have a full and heavy backpack that you have been carrying around, the rest of this book will give you the tools to start to unload those bricks and move back into more trust, love, and connection with your partner.

Though we are sure you now understand the importance of not carrying around a "heavy backpack of resentment" in your relationship, there is one other major reason that avoiding conflicts (aka: "picking your battles") is a destructive thing to do. Withholding your needs, desires, or wants from your partner primarily comes from the fear of rejection. You might read that and think *I'm not afraid of my partner.* Even though you might not consciously be aware of a fear right now, being rejected is an underlying fear we all have. This basic fear influences all of us in some way, shape, or form.

According to Maslow's Hierarchy of Needs, the level three need is to belong and be accepted. It's almost primal. Just like you don't have to think about avoiding getting hit by an oncoming bus (because your body would just move), you don't think about how to avoid feeling rejected because it's an automatic reaction. This need to belong and be accepted is even more heightened if you're with someone that you really love and want to be with for the remainder of your life. Your brain's programming would make you think it's safer not to share something that might upset your partner and could lead to rejection. Jot this down . . . your brain is designed for you to survive moment by moment, not necessarily to do the things that will help you thrive in the longer term.

This is actually a good thing when it comes to avoiding actual dangerous situations, but not when it comes to having a more open, connected, and understanding relationship. You will have to listen more to your heart and intuition rather than your brain when leaning into initially difficult situations, which at times will make your brain say "this is not a good idea, this is not safe, this is going to cause an argument." You are going to have to risk putting your heart and soul on the line and trust that you are still safe and loved. Your relationship is not something you have to try and survive. Highlight this goal for your relationship: *create an environment where we both are safe and accepted as we share anything with each other.*

A step to dissolving the belief that you should "pick your battles" is to recognize that you don't need to fear being rejected by your partner. (Don't worry, later on we'll address what to do if you do think your partner rejects things you say or if you think you're outspoken and it goes nowhere).

The last reason why "picking your battles" is terrible advice to follow is because anyone telling you to pick your battles already relates to having to "battle" someone in a relationship. When there is a battle to fight, doesn't that also mean there must be a winner and a loser? Why would you ever want to have a relationship built on the foundation that one of you will be the winner and that one of you will be the loser? That certainly doesn't sound like a great position to put your partner in.

We really searched and searched around this topic, and we just couldn't find any set of wedding vows that went like this: "I promise to love, honor, and cherish you . . . and when we have a battle I promise to feel sorry that you had to be the loser!" Of course we are taking some creative liberty to add some humor to this point, but it is our stance that you shouldn't set yourselves up to always have someone feel that they lose in the relationship. A partnership that wants to be successful for all the years to come finds a way to have both partners win as a team! When you are a team (insert any sports team here), it's the entire team that wins, right? It's not just one individual person. We are not looking to set any unrealistic or overly optimistic expectations here. We know there will be challenges and seasons of your relationship when you don't feel things are going your way. You might be in a season where you do not feel you are winning as a team at all. But isn't it better, even in those moments, to "lose" knowing you were a part of a team that at least did its best and that you were in it together?

You should not have to "pick your battles" because you're afraid to feel like you always "lose" the battle or even because you worry about your partner's reaction. If you do happen to find this is still the case in your current dynamic, then you're going to love what we teach about emotional triggers on page 45. But for now, take a moment to reflect on the times in your relationship when you might have started to withhold sharing certain things because you worried about your partner's reaction, or that it would turn into an escalated disagreement. Here are some good, reflective questions you could journal about:

- Was there a certain turning point in my relationship when disagreements started to escalate, or has it been like this since the beginning?
- Are there any thoughts, emotions, ideas, or needs that I have withheld from my partner lately?
- In what ways do I worry that what I say won't be accepted or that I'll be rejected?

We highly encourage you to do some silent reflection on these questions. Then, talk to your partner through them when they can listen to you non-defensively.

THE "HAPPY WIFE, HAPPY LIFE" BELIEF

This saying must have been created by someone in the 1700s who had already suppressed and stuffed away any sense of connection and gumption for the relationship. All out of fear of upsetting their wife and the "ensuing retribution" they would incur. They then took it upon themselves to spread the word to their friends down at the saloon, and it caught on like wildfire. Just imagine for a second how that conversation went: "Kind sirs, I discovered thy way of being happy and not getting in a heated scuffle with thine wife. Keepeth her happy." "Tell us more," they said. "Well, just don't tell her anything that will make her angry. Then thou shalt agree to everything she says, even if thine aren't going to do it." Everyone then replied, "Ahhh yes, thee art a genius! We shall follow thy path too." Then it was passed on to their kids, who passed it on to their kids, etc., till you then were lucky enough to hear this horrible advice.

Joking aside, the idea of "happy wife, happy life" doesn't *really* feel right in the long-run for most couples. It might feel like a safe bet to keep things cool, calm, and collected but it ultimately leads to neither person really feeling deeply fulfilled. Most of our clients say that they actually despise this saying because they feel:

- It puts their partner in a passive, non-participatory state.
- It forces them into a dominant/masculine role when they are not choosing to be.
- Isolated and alone with an unequal balance in making decisions.
- That they don't ever get to *really know* their partner's true likes/dislikes or needs.

For those of you that inherited this outdated belief to just succumb to whatever your partner wants in order to keep the peace and avoid causing any problems, please understand that it puts your partner in a position they don't want to be in. In fact, they really want to know what your opinion is, what matters to you, and how you feel about a situation. Sure, there might be a small percentage of partners who want everything to go their way and to make all the decisions in the relationship, but that's really not the majority of people.

Your partner wants to truly *know* you, even if they don't agree with you. It can feel quite boring to just hear things like, "yes, whatever you want, honey." That might be nice to hear once in a while, but if that is the dominant response it can be really frustrating and isolating.

If you tend to be more of the reserved type of person that has tried to avoid conflict by not expressing yourself proactively, worry not. On page 151 we'll dive into the four communication personality types and how to speak up to express your needs and wants in a constructive way.

In closing out this belief, we encourage you to switch the belief that your partner is happiest if you go along with what they want. That might be nice on their birthday or here and there, but not all the time. You two will feel more connected and freer with each other if your happiness comes from knowing and understanding each other. Your opinion *does* matter to them, and you'll learn throughout the book about how to share it in a non-confrontational way.

THE "IT'S BETTER TO SWEEP THINGS UNDER THE RUG" BELIEF

The only thing you should ever sweep under the rug is dog hair or dirt from outside. (But why on earth would you do that?) Bad joke aside, "sweeping things under the rug" is an idiom that builds up into a tripping hazard later on in many relationships. This is the third outdated belief that is not serving your relationship and probably doing unknown damage already.

Over time, if you figuratively sweep things under the rug in your relationship, it builds up in a pile of "emotional junk" and resentments that create more distance from your partner. In this situation, the underlying intent is *not* to cause a conflict. If you're being honest, many of us at some point have said or heard from our partner: "it's not a big deal, just move past it already." We have heard this enough times from clients that we know what this statement really means. (If we are being honest too, we have done this ourselves enough times to know this next statement is true.) Using a statement like this with your partner is a deflection from actually feeling the emotion that is either there for you personally, or that is being felt by your partner.

> When you say "just get over it already," what you are really saying is "I don't have the emotional capacity to feel this emotion right now."

So, if you now can catch yourself when you are about to use this phrase, instead pause and think to yourself *what emotion am I avoiding acknowledging or feeling*?

When you say "This isn't a big deal, just get over it," you are making a one-sided assumption. This isn't a big deal to whom? *You*! Isn't that being a little selfish? Just because it isn't a big deal to you doesn't mean it's not important to your partner. In fact, because you are having this conversion in which your partner *is* feeling emotion, doesn't it show you that it does mean something to them? (Just so we are all on the same page here, the answer is *yes*!) So, sweeping it under the rug isn't really getting rid of anything. In the short-term it may seem like a good idea to avoid conflict once again, but in fact letting it linger builds the potential for decreased assertiveness, low self-confidence, and resentment. Which to reiterate again, the Gottman Institute has identified resentment as one of the four major causes of a deteriorating relationship, and a surefire way to predict an inevitable divorce.[3]

Okay, that was a deep section, go ahead and stand up and shake it out if you need to. While reading this section you might have thought to yourself *but what if the event in question really isn't that big*

---

3 Gottman, John M. *The Seven Principles for Making Marriage Work*. New York: Three Rivers Press, 1999.

of a deal after all, and when do you know if you should just forgive and let it go without talking about it? There are times where it's not about sweeping it under the rug, and your partner might have been having what we call a "human blip" moment. Oxford Languages defines a blip as "an unexpected, minor, and temporary deviation from a general trend." In other words, it's being human and having an "off" moment when you or your partner didn't show up at your best. You made a small mistake, a lapse in judgement, or just didn't pay that much attention to a given situation.

If you find yourself being hyper-critical or hyper-sensitive, it's worth identifying moments where compassion could be helpful in "human blip" moments. For example, if your partner had a rough day at work and their tone of voice isn't the most loving, offer them a hug rather than criticizing them or attacking back. When your partner is having a human moment, it can be much more effective to take a loving action rather than giving verbal feedback or pointing out something they are doing wrong.

You may be wondering *how do I know if a given situation is something that needs to be talked about and addressed, or if I can chalk it up as a human blip moment?* Here are a few questions to help make the differentiation:

1. Is this a *recurring* behavior of my partner that continues to hurt or frustrate me?
   - If yes, continue to question 2.
   - If no, it could be a human blip moment that could use compassion.
2. Is it frustrating to me because I *just want to control* the behavior, or because this situation is just not going my way?
   - If yes, try to release the need to control how small things are done, and consider it a human blip moment.
   - If no, continue to question 3.

3. Is there strong emotion because this is *truly important* to me?
  - If yes, this is a conversation to address with your partner in a calm manner leveraging the skills you learn in the upcoming chapters.
  - If no, it could be a human blip moment.

Remember that if you sweep things under the rug for the sake of avoiding a conflict in the short-term, the odds lend to it being a bigger and more intimidating issue in the long-term. You know the saying, "what you resist, persists"? Well the challenge, frustration, or feeling you have will continue to persist if you resist talking about it with your partner.

As you two work on this proactive level of communication, you'll get more comfortable distinguishing between a human blip moment and the moments when you should have a deeper conversation with your partner to prevent any "emotional junk" from piling up. Until then, commit to talking about important conversations and cultivating a safe space for you to be able to share anything in your heart and mind.

THE "CONFLICT IS BAD, AND SOMETHING IS WRONG HERE" BELIEF

Before we go into the more empowering beliefs about conflict in the next chapter, we wanted to address one more outdated belief to confront. It's a very pervasive and unconscious belief that leads you to either avoid conflict or escalate it to the point of an Argument Hangover. And that belief is "if we are fighting, that means something is wrong."

Now, we're going to say something pretty bold here: a large percentage of divorces could be avoided if the belief "something is wrong here" didn't exist in their minds. Well, sure, some divorces happen after a couple really tried to work through things to get on the same page, but didn't succeed. But, actually, many more of them end up being the result of *not* fighting enough. We hear individual clients say left and right, "I had no idea my partner wasn't happy and all of a sudden they want a divorce." Or, "we just avoided things and didn't talk about them, and they grew to be so big we couldn't find our way out." It's those statements that have led to us discovering this unfortunate silent disease in relationships. To say it one additional way, it can also sound like "this shouldn't be happening." You can have this idea in your mind that a conflict should not be happening in your relationship, and that is what leads to you thinking *something is wrong here*. Even if you are nowhere near thinking about divorce, this belief likely still exists for you if you find yourself resisting conflict.

So, first things first, conflict *should* be happening. Yes, you can take a sigh of relief. Conflict is a sign that you're alive, you're human, and that you're growing and progressing as a couple. It's also a sign that you're having *real* conversations, and not just talking about surface level things in life like your to-do lists or what you want to watch on TV.

As counterintuitive as it may seem, we actually want you to fight *more*—of course, using the healthy tools we'll share in the coming chapters. But when we say fight, we mean fight *for* your relationship and not against each other. We want you to confront the tough stuff, we want you to grapple with different feelings and challenges that come up between you two. It's in these moments that you learn even more about each other.

Don't avoid conflict. Don't avoid seeing your partner feel different emotions that you might perceive as "bad" (like being mad, sad, or hurt). It's okay if either of you have moments of feeling confronted or experiencing unpleasant emotions. Don't avoid the really uncomfortable moments . . . because if you stick through it, you two can actually become stronger than ever.

One of the reasons couples say they want to "work on conflict resolution" is actually because they resist it and want conflict to disappear altogether. If you didn't resist conflict, you wouldn't get so upset if they disagreed with you. You wouldn't hold back your feelings to the point where it boiled up to a bigger problem, and you wouldn't get to the point of wanting to walk out of the room because you didn't like how the argument felt. Those are all subtle signs of resisting conflict.

On the other hand, if you embraced conflict, you would listen calmly if your partner shared a different view from you. You would tackle a challenge between you two right away, instead of letting it linger. And you would have a shorter Argument Hangover because you two embraced the tough conversation consciously.

Here are two ways to look at it:

- When you think *something is wrong here*, you are resisting conflict because it feels like it shouldn't be happening. Which only leads to creating more distance in the relationship.
- When you can think *there's nothing wrong here*, you are embracing conflict because you know it's a natural part of a relationship. Which is the way you can get more connected.

Let's go back to one of our previous statements about wanting you to fight more. What we mean is that your partnership will actually be more authentic and unbreakable if you confront the challenges right as they come up. You could even talk about possible conflicts that might happen in the future and how you will handle them! The type of healthy conflict you'll learn about in this book is based on the belief that "there's nothing wrong here," and this is a beautiful opportunity for your relationship to grow. You might want to read this part twice—conflict can feel very personal to your relationship, like it must be a flaw between you two. But that is not true. Our entire motto behind our work with couples is "behind every challenge is a missing skill."

We know there were a lot of new ideas and a special focus on our part to knock down some old beliefs that we invite you to let go of in your relationship. In the end, if there is even just one outdated relationship belief that you choose to upgrade from our suggestions, it will bring you that much closer to fighting smarter and avoiding common communication pitfalls that lead to hangovers. To do that, each chapter will have a "Game Plan" section at the end so that you can decide on which action to take next in your relationship. Then, check off the boxes as you complete each step.

YOUR GAME PLAN

- Reflect on any outdated beliefs that might be contributing to how you perceive or handle conflict with your partner.
- Identify if you have been carrying around any resentments from avoiding conflict.
- Discuss with your partner if you notice that you two have a pattern of "sweeping things under the rug" or distracting yourselves from resolving them.
- Start to distinguish the things that truly do matter to you and need to be discussed versus the "human blip" moments.
- Bring some light energy to moments where one of you has a "human blip" moment, and bring compassion.

You can fight smarter and shorten the Argument Hangover by removing outdated beliefs you unknowingly have about conflicts.

3

TURNING CONFLICT
INTO A GOOD THING

"We cannot solve our problems with the same level of thinking that we created them in."

—Albert Einstein

When you see the word "conflict," what is it that you immediately think or feel? You probably think of conflict first of all as something that's tough, something that's going to be challenging, difficult to get through, or an obstacle to overcome. Especially if you and your partner have a bad track record for how your disagreements have gone, the idea of conflict can make you feel anxious or worried, and want to avoid or at least get past it as fast as you can. If this is the case, you most likely believe that a conflict involves something you have to fight against. You may view conflict now as some sort of battle in which you are either going to win or lose.

If any part of this rings true for you, you are in good company, as thousands of couples have shared their negative feelings toward conflict. It really is no surprise that couples try to avoid conflict because honestly who wants to battle against their partner, put in all that energy, just to end up feeling like you've been defeated? Even if you did come out as the winner, is it really any benefit when the person you love now feels like they have just lost? As we described in the previous chapter, you likely have related to conflict as "something is wrong here," which makes you resist it.

Jordan in our couples community asked a great question: "how do you re-train your brain not to shut down during conflicts and to embrace healthy communication to resolve conflicts?" It's a powerful question and one that is becoming more and more common. What if you could totally transform the way you relate to conflict and, dare we say it, see (and feel) conflict within your relationship as a good thing? What if you didn't resist conflict at all?

EVERYTHING HAS AN OPPOSITE

First things first, let's get rid of the entire belief and energy-draining feeling of seeing conflict as some sort of battle with a winner and a loser. A conflict is simply the result of two opposing (or different) views, but it does not have to be an event that pits you against each other. If you really take the time to think through this next statement as you read, it can change everything. Everything in life must first have an opposite to it. In fact, you have never actually experienced anything without first experiencing its opposite. Some real-world examples are: You would not know what light was without having experienced darkness. You would not know what warm was if not for having experienced cold. You would not know which way was "up" if not referenced to "down."

Having an opposite means having a reference to compare one thing to another and it all has to do with your perception. It's all in the way you see it. In the examples of darkness and cold, these are perceptions with your outward facing senses. You have experienced many opposites this way, and we will refer to these opposites from here on as "contrast." You are likely very familiar with photos being posted on social media. Of all the thousands of posts, what is it that makes any one of them stand out from the rest? It's the use of contrast, isn't it? You wouldn't notice the brilliance of color from a sunrise for instance if not for the dark contrast of a mountain ridge.

So, from this point, remember that contrast is necessary for you to really notice or experience anything! In fact, how would you really experience the blissful moments with your partner without having had contrasting challenging moments?

Now, let's talk about contrast in relation to how conflicts between you and your partner are experienced. What you are about to notice is that the principle of contrast is still in reality the same, and is just as necessary if you want to progress in your relationship. What has happened unfortunately is that you have distorted this contrast (or as you currently experience it, as a conflict) and made it into something that is bad and that you want to avoid. It's time to shift your perception and see and leverage conflicts in your relationship as a benefit! We don't know about you, since we are not there reading beside you, but we certainly are excited about this!

CONFLICT IS SIMPLY TWO DIFFERENT VIEWS

This is the first important aspect of a conflict being seen as a good and necessary thing. In a sense, a conflict first starts with two different views. Maybe for you and your partner it's two different ways to handle finances, what type of house to live in, or how to parent kids. Fundamentally there's nothing overly significant, harsh, or difficult about that, right? You can have an opposing perspective from your partner and not fight over it. You are always going to see things differently however slightly than your partner. Heck, like we have already covered, you are bound to perceive things somewhat differently than everyone else on the planet, so there is no need to try and convince someone to see things exactly how you do!

Seeing things differently, or having contrast in your relationship, allows for something new to be seen or experienced. It actually allows for you, as partners, to become aware of a new desire that you weren't aware of before. This by itself is a beautiful thing: that you could be living life one way and then all of a sudden come to the realization of a new desired way to make your relationship even better! So, contrast is just a change in your awareness. A conflict in your relationship can just be the continuous way you become aware of a new desire that had not been there before.

Conflicts at their core are events in your relationship that show you the difference between what you do *not* want in your relationship versus what you actually do want. This is the way in which your relationship grows and progresses. If you didn't have the ability to see what you do not want within your relationship, you would have no way of figuring out what you really do want. Just like without any dark contrast, you would never know what light was!

> The only real problem with conflict is remaining focused on the aspects of your relationship that you don't want and never using the contrast to discover what you want next!

Okay, that may have been a big concept so let's see how this plays out in your day-to-day life. We are always about making complex ideas practical and implementable! What good is anything if you are unable to use it in your own life, right? The initial conflict between you both might seem to pit you against each other over topics like how much money you have been spending, how critical you are when you talk to each other, the lack of intimacy, dissatisfaction with your career, the amount of happiness in your relationship, or not being on the same page with your spiritual beliefs. This can feel unsettling just because of the uncertainty it brings up. You don't really want to have these areas of your relationship continue to go the same way they always have. Yet you feel unclear or even afraid to make a change, which can cause stress or feelings of uncertainty about the future. But remember . . . this is not the point to focus on. You are going to change from focusing on what you do not want any more to focusing on what it is that you *do* want. We repeat, you cannot experience lasting change, aka what you do want, by focusing on what you do not want.

Now is the opportunity to come together and clarify the new desire you have for the future. The first step is to break the contrast down into its specific core area of your relationship. If in the moment it is becoming very clear that you and your partner are seeing things differently, this is not the time to fight over who is right or wrong because then you will miss the whole point. Instead, clarify with each other what core area of your relationship this conflict is about. Later on we will cover all core areas in detail, but for now decide which area this conflict falls into:

- Communication
- Family
- Financial
- Mental
- Physical
- Professional
- Sexual
- Social
- Spiritual

Categorizing your conflict into an area will help you shorten the Argument Hangover period as well as keep it from escalating. It will also allow you to simplify your conversations and bring in the perspective that you only have a conflict in this one area, rather than a general "we have a problem" mentality. This can also help you realize that many other areas are working well for you, which may de-escalate the current level of emotion you're feeling from your conflict.

The next step is to clarify what you do want, from what this contrast is showing you that you do not want. Let's take a look at some of the conflict statements from above and see how you can use them to your advantage. There are two questions to ask your partner (or for them to ask you) when you get into these contrasting situations. These two questions are:

1. Why is that important for us?
2. What do you want instead?

Here is an example of how one conversation could go:

Partner: "I'm so tired of the way you have been talking to me and criticizing me."

You: "It sounds like you are upset about the area of our communication?"

Partner: "Well yes, I guess I would say that." (Notice how asking a question about the area already kept the emotion from escalating and putting you into an Argument Hangover period.)

You: "Okay, so why is that important for us?" (Notice the use of "us" instead of "you" to keep you on the same team.)

Partner: "I don't really know about for us, but it's important to me (pause as they are thinking) because it makes me feel that you do not value what I have to say."

You: "What do you want instead?"

Partner: "I would like to share new ideas I have with you so that we can be more on the same page and feel we are equal partners in making decisions."

The new desire that got revealed from a moment of conflict: Feel more connected and be equal partners! (Isn't that a good thing?) Here is an example of how a second conversation could go:

You: "I just paid the credit card bills and I can't believe how much money you spent last month."

Partner: "Okay, so this seems like you are upset about the area of our finances?" (Notice how first categorizing into the area of finances can help keep the emotion from immediately escalating, especially around a stressful area like money.)

You: "Yes, that's right."

Partner: "Well, why is that so important for us?"

You: "Well (notice that you pause for reflection rather than let the emotion carry you off into an Argument Hangover), it's important for us not to spend so much routinely so we can better track how much we have."

Partner: "What do you want instead?"

You: "Good question (another pause for conscious reflection), I would like for us to have allocated amounts each month for expense, fun, and travel. I really would like to travel more with you and see more of the world."

The new desire that got revealed from a moment of conflict: Have financial structure to be able to see more of the world together! (Isn't that a good thing?) Take a moment to see which specific words were used to keep this conversation from escalating into a fight. Asking the question "why is that important to us?" is powerful because it reminds you that the only reason one or both of you might be upset is because something matters to either of you. Wow, your partner cares . . . how cool is that?

Just a quick side note as we know the topic of money can cause stress. If by reading that last example you thought *that was too unrealistic because my partner isn't reading this book with me and would react much more harshly*, we admit that just reading this book on your own is not going to fix everything. Some conversations that have a lot of past history are going to take more time to implement the right skills together, and may need help facilitating at first. That's why we have additional resources for you to get more guidance and support with our courses, workshops, and coaching on page X.

The goal is to see that there are two sides to every conflict. But remember, we are not talking about the two sides being your perspective versus your partner's. The two sides are what you do not want and using that to get clarity about what you do want. There are always these two sides in every argument, and its benefit to you will depend on which you focus on! Like two sides of a coin, on one side is what you don't want, and on the other side is what you do want.

**front of the
coin:
what you DON'T want**

**back of the
coin:
what you DO want**

which one are you focusing on?

Since we provided you just the two examples of new desires for finances and communication, we provided more examples in the table below. You can choose to do this as another exercise if you write down all of the conflicts (or even just frustrations) you have with your partner in the left-hand column. (That will likely be the easy part because it's what you've been focusing on more often.) Then, in the right-hand column, write what you do want with as much detail as you can think of.

As you can see, conflict really is a good thing because it offers clarity on what you want as a couple! You can't achieve something if you don't know the goal. You just have to let go of continuing to focus on the left-hand column (what you don't want) and focus more on the right-hand column (what you do want).

Here is a personal example for us even as we were writing this book together. Guess what came up between us . . . conflicts! There were a few days that we had tough conversations about the book that

What you don't want in this conflict:	What you do want:
Intimacy: I don't want to be the only one that initiates our intimacy and I do not want it to only be once per month.	I would like us both to initiate intimacy equally and have it happen at least twice each week. I want to feel more desired by my partner.
Professional: I don't want you to work in this field any longer and I don't want you to be gone so much each week.	I want us to feel more fulfilled with work, have more time to spend together as a family, and earn even more money.
Communication: I'm not happy about the way we talk to each other. I do not want us to blame and point fingers at each other so much.	I would like to feel heard, seen, and understood. I would like to have peaceful conversations and learn more about each other.
Spiritual: I don't want to argue about our spiritual beliefs and have separate practices.	I would like spirituality to be something that we connect on and have more meaningful conversations about.
Add your examples here:	*Add your examples here:*

led each of us to getting upset, needing to have our own space, and even taking a day off that was planned for writing. The conflicts that came up were in the form of opposing views on each other's writing style: about how *not* conversational a section was that Aaron wrote, that there was too much logic or scientific references to make it relatable for you the reader. In that moment it felt like a personal attack, criticism, and that writing this book was not fun. Though this came up (how interesting that we were writing this exact chapter about conflicts) we kept remembering that conflicts were meant to show us the contrast between what we had currently written, and what kind of writing was going to produce the most relatable and impactful book for you! That being said, was every single moment of writing this book fun for us? No. There were moments we felt criticized or put down by each other. But we did not let emotion escalate to the point of doing any damage to our connection, we didn't have these upset periods last very long, and we effectively navigated around any Argument Hangovers. The result of each moment of contrast was that we wrote better and better for each draft. The result (if we do say so ourselves) is the best possible book we could have put out! Conflict was in fact a great thing. You can leverage conflicts the same way in your relationship, to produce the best possible outcome for you both!

Maybe you have heard the following phrase before, maybe not. If not, we are happy that you can hear from us! True intimacy is "in-to-me-you-see." Intimacy is not just the physical intimacy you have together; it is also emotional intimacy. The truth is, the deeper your emotional connection is, the better your physical intimacy will be! But your emotional intimacy only goes as far as you are willing to let your partner "see into you." Can you be even more open, honest, and authentic about your true feelings, the emotions that you feel, and the things that cause you to feel hurt or upset? It's an intimate experience when you reveal your true self. The more you dive into these conflicts and discover just why you were upset, why it was important to you, and what you now desire for your relationship, the deeper your intimacy will go. From here on out, think of conflicts in your relationship just like a gold miner thinks of digging for gold. You don't ever strike it rich just digging on the surface. You have to dig down deep to find the real gold.

WHEN CONFLICT FEELS LIKE AN ATTACK

It is our hope at this point that you already feel a shift or a softening of beliefs about conflict between you and your partner. Rather than avoiding or stressing about it being a battle against the two of you, your idea of conflict can be one of positive anticipation. Not that you are looking forward to having a conflict with your partner, but you are more optimistic that the next conflict will give you both more clarity! Let's be straight-up here, they will still come up. The goal of a relationship is not to be conflict-free because you would miss out on all the clarity, learning, and growth we just covered.

To be able to approach your next conflict in this new way, it is important to at least know why some things happen the way they do. You may still be wondering about why fights have gotten out of control for you in the past, and why having a difference of opinion could have felt like such a personal attack. Here's why. In these moments, what you are feeling is the tension between your partner's perspective and a belief that you have. During this conversation you are having with your partner, they have verbalized their view on the subject at hand, but you do not believe it to be right. Their view does not match up to what you believe to be true for yourself. This belief you have is so true to you and held so tightly, that you experience this conflict (remember, it's really just opposing views) as actually attacking who you are as a person. In your mind you think that your belief is who you are.

So, when something comes in opposition to the belief (or identity) of who you are, this event becomes something you must fight for. In this moment your belief is almost indistinguishable from who you are as an individual. So when someone judges, disregards, puts down, tries to dominate, or devalues this belief, it feels like they are doing this to you or more so against you. To lose this battle would mean that what you had believed so strongly was actually wrong, that you are wrong. This can feel like a death of sorts. A death of an aspect of your personality or identity, an aspect of who you are as a person. (Yes, we get it, this feels very emotional and significant to try and keep your identity from dying.) But, wait a minute, let's examine that. Is this really the case? Are your beliefs really who you are?

After that last paragraph, it might be worth standing up again and shaking it off. Move around a bit and shift the energy! That was a big statement and realization. You might have started to relate to a particular circumstance in your own relationship where you have been feeling an attack on who you are and on your self-identity. You may have even started to feel some of the emotion that we were referring to. It's really powerful to notice your own personal thoughts about a conflict you have, or thoughts about your partner. Do you believe they are irresponsible, disrespectful, or untrustworthy? What do you believe about yourself? Do you believe you should never be questioned, that you are always right, or that your perspective is more important?

It's this combination of your tightly held beliefs about yourself (and the emotion that is tied to it as you will learn in the next chapter about triggers) that keeps you feeling like you have to fight for your life when it comes to certain areas of your relationship. Even when this conversation is with your lover, your partner, your spouse, or someone that you have committed to sharing your life with. At some point you will reflect on an argument and think *how could I have said those things, how could I have gotten so angry, how did I let it go that far?* It's because you were in pure survival mode trying not to let yourself (your tightly held belief and identity) be killed off. You were battling to protect yourself. One of the biggest results from this book will be to realize that what you were fighting so hard for was not even really you.

If you can separate a belief from the identity of who you are as a person, you can greatly reduce the amount of emotion and need to fight when a conflict arises with your partner. Here comes the big reveal: Your beliefs are just the thoughts that you think most often! When you believe something, it is of course true for you in that moment, but these beliefs are not typically universal truths, only personal truths. They are just what you have thought most often, and probably for a long period of time.

Beliefs are something that you can change. If you thought differently about something (like your partner, or even a belief about yourself) frequently enough, it would become a new belief. It's not necessarily easy, as you will come to find out, but with practice you can change them to be anything that you want. Isn't that amazing? Since you can change them, they are not something you have to fight for your life to hold on to. Instead, you can be more fluid and freer when you and your partner discuss different beliefs. Doesn't that make you feel more relaxed and calmer, not as fearful or scared to have a conflict?

Let's take a quick pause for reflection. What have you been thinking about most in your relationship and what has that made you feel? If you think that your partner doesn't value your opinion, does not respect you, or is disappointed in you, we're sorry to say but this is all on you! You have let this become your belief and reality about them. How can someone ever do anything right when this is the belief you have about them? There is not much chance of improving the relationship from there.

Instead, if you start to change your thoughts to be about what you are grateful for about your partner, the ways in which they support and show you love, that will start to become your new belief. Almost magically you will start to see them show up more and more as a match to that reality. Your beliefs actually reflect your most dominant attitude toward your partner. So, whether you choose to have thoughts that are positive or negative, your attitude is going to be a match. It's what you have allowed yourself to think about your partner most often that influences your attitude toward them.

We do not want to oversimplify the importance of developing your ability to challenge your beliefs. It is a difficult thing to do at first because your beliefs are things that you think are 100 percent true. The problem is, many of us don't think much differently than our parents did or the culture we grew up in, and we often fail to see how these thought processes can impact our adult relationships. Many of us don't ever challenge our own beliefs to find out if what we have been believing is actually true, or is just true for us.

Putting it into perspective, you normally fight others when they challenge your beliefs, don't you? You don't have to look very far into today's society to see that to be true. Look at how often people fight one another, often for the sake of their own made-up beliefs that they are unwilling to question or rethink if they are really worth holding on to.

Typically, this continues until some major life event happens like a sickness, death, coming up against a really hard financial time, or a pandemic (like we happen to be experiencing during the time of this book). Once this happens, it rapidly changes your perspective! It's funny how fast a belief can change, even when it was held to be absolutely true for so long. There are two main ways to change your beliefs, and it's through repetition and emotion. Repetition over the course of your life is how the majority of your beliefs got there in the first place. Yet when a major crisis or life event happens, it's the surge of high emotion that quickly shifts your perspective. This is how beliefs can change quickly, which in turn changes your actions, and consequently the results that happen for you.

It comes down to whether you decide to change your thoughts and your corresponding beliefs. You could decide to make this choice before something major happens in your life. And wouldn't that be better? Wouldn't you rather it be a choice of yours and not an indirect result of when something bad happens? Unfortunately, many couples let their beliefs ruin their marriage, and wait until the pain of a divorce causes them to shift their beliefs. Most people just don't know this. But being open to questioning your beliefs can change how you fight with your partner and truly leverage conflicts into the clear benefit they can be for your relationship.

THE REAL BENEFIT OF CONFLICT

When you start to see conflict as just two different views (that can both be valid), you can be grateful for the clarity that you are receiving from any event. You will actually come together with your partner and say, "Oh, wow, we now see something new that we want or desire for our relationship that we never saw before!" Allow that contrast to bring about this clarity of new actions for you to move forward to the life that you want to live together. It can allow you to be more connected, intimate, have more opportunities, wealth, friends, and even more influence. Look at any period in your relationship, in your life, or any time in history when a positive change, evolution, or improvement came about. Didn't it come about first within this new definition of conflict? There must be a contrast for you both to do anything to change or improve. When you face this together, all of a sudden, all conflict can be seen as a benefit!

As Albert Einstein even said, "we cannot solve our problems at the same level of thinking that we created them in." It is conflict that brings about the opportunity to change and upgrade your level of thinking. It's this new level of thinking that will reveal new, different, and creative solutions to anything you face in your relationship. When you do that together as a true team, seeking to first understand each other's perspective and not feel you have to fight to have your perspective win, you not only shorten the Argument Hangover but you keep from falling into the same destructive pitfalls that do more damage to your connection. In turn you are able to face any challenge that arises, not to survive in spite of it, but to thrive because of it!

Conflicts allow for a new/better/different perspective and corresponding solution to be uncovered or revealed. Without this process you are stuck with more of the same. With the same outlook, you will never see or believe what's possible, only what is predictable, and take the actions that keep producing the same results. Remember from the first chapter: it's the progressive realization of your worthy ideal that is the basis for success. You will never be successful in your relationship if you are not willing to see things in a new way. Your ability to see things newly comes from your willingness to have conflicts and not avoid them. Of course, you and your partner will have different ways of seeing things! Don't be so rigid that your view is right and theirs is wrong. Examine your perspective, their perspective, and discover a brand-new third perspective *together* that you never even saw before on your own, that is even more of a benefit to the relationship. This raises your level of thinking! From this level, you will find better solutions to any problem that you face in your relationship.

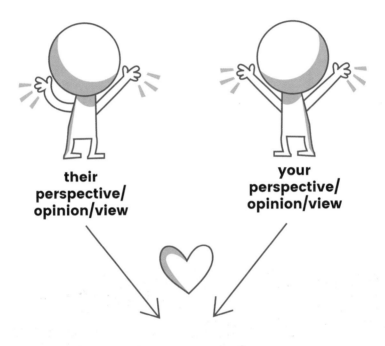

**their
perspective/
opinion/view**

**your
perspective/
opinion/view**

**a 3rd even better perspective/solution for the
benefit of your relationship!**

YOUR GAME PLAN

Here are some new ideas that will help shift your beliefs about conflicts in your relationship. Write these (or similar statements) down every time you have a conflict come up in the next two weeks. You will see that after repetition, you will begin to see, feel, and believe that conflicts in your relationship really are a good thing. Then, categorize any conflicts you have and uncover what you do want.

- Even though I'm feeling strong emotion right now, I know this will eventually show me an equally positive solution.
- The two of us can always come up with a better solution than I could on my own.
- This conflict is allowing me to gain more clarity on what I do want for our relationship.
- Categorize a conflict into one of the specific core areas of the relationship.
- Write down the side of what you do not want and the side of what you do want.

You can fight smarter and shorten the Argument Hangover by understanding what conflicts really are and how they benefit you.

4

EMOTIONAL TRIGGERS AND THEIR IMPACT

"When you squeeze an orange, orange juice comes out—because that's what's inside. When you are squeezed, what comes out is what is inside."

—Dr. Wayne W. Dyer

This opening quote by Dr. Wayne Dyer is one of our personal favorites. Of course, because it has an air of humor and lightheartedness to it, but also because it is one of those reminders that has allowed us to shorten our own Argument Hangovers. As we previously covered, one of the biggest things that causes you to experience the Argument Hangover is your belief that a disagreement is a time to fight and battle against each other, rather than stay on the same team, stay connected, and find creative solutions collaboratively together. This is why the hangover period ends up leading to more damage than the initial "event" that caused it. We will refer to these events as your triggers. You will actually feel empowered by this change in terminology because it allows you to take control of your own reactions and role in causing the Argument Hangover, rather than continue to see events as outside circumstances you have no control over. When you don't feel you have control over something, it has the potential to put you in a frustrated, resentful, and victim mentality—and you obviously don't want to live there.

Think about this opening quote again: "When you squeeze an orange, orange juice comes out—because that's what's inside. When you are squeezed, what comes out is what is inside." Orange juice is of course the only thing you would ever expect to come out if you squeeze an orange. You would never expect lemon juice or apple juice to come out, that would be quite the surprise indeed! It's obvious to you that the only juice to come out of a squeezed orange is orange juice. But you might not have connected that analogy to yourself yet. Wayne Dyer always did such an amazing job painting this picture for what this has to do with you as an individual person. In this chapter, we want to look at what happens when "someone squeezes you," aka puts pressure on you.

In your relationship, what type of events cause you to feel pressure? Is there a specific area of your relationship (like finances or intimacy) that when brought up by your partner, causes you to feel uncomfortable, sensitive, or emotional? Maybe you feel caught off guard when this conversation is brought up, so you get immediately defensive, hurt, sad, or even overwhelmed. This could be because your partner says things like, "What is this $100 expense from last week? You don't show me affection anymore. Can't you help with the dishes more often? We don't have sex very often." Or even something similar to these submissions from couples in our community:

- "No triggers with my new husband. Ex-husband triggered me by his insistence that I change. He was like a supervisor waiting to write me up for corrective action."
- "When I'm told that I'm overreacting or that something is all in my head."
- "Using the expressions 'all the time,' 'never,' or 'always.'"
- "Being asked why something is done a certain way. The question feels rhetorical, and is asked because it's different than how they would have done it."
- "I need my space."

Think now about what statements/questions/remarks trigger you so they're present as you go through the rest of the chapter. When these events happen, it's almost automatic that you feel emotion begin to rise. We call this a trigger because an emotional trigger arises any time your partner starts a conversation that puts pressure on you.

Your immediate reaction could be "my partner is the one that brought this up, and they are causing me to feel _____" (fill in the blank with the emotion you typically feel in these moments)! But as Dr. Dyer's analogy suggests, it is not because of your partner at all! It's not because they brought this up at a bad time, or necessarily the tone or manner in which they brought this up. It's because that emotion was inside already!

**being triggered is like being poked
in a sensitive spot, and what comes
out is what was already inside**

Okay, take a short pause to check on your emotions right now. We know that statement initially seems absurd. Your mind probably wants to reject that idea right out of the gate. You could feel defensive to this claim because you are not the one that is bringing this conversation up, so your reaction isn't your fault. It's the way they said it that caused you to react that way, right? Or it's because they brought it up at a bad time, after you had a really bad day at work. But this is not the time to pass blame, and it's not even the time to feel bad about your past reactions. This is actually empowering because the responsibility is all on you and is in your control. We'll dive much more into a new way to look at responsibility in the coming chapters, but for now we just want you to see responsibility as your ability to respond.

Going back to the orange juice analogy . . . just as the orange juice comes out of the orange every single time, and never anything else, what comes out of you in these moments of being triggered is not a result of your partner, but because that emotion was already inside of you. Think about this: If a stranger walked up to you and said "hey, you have weird green hair," you likely would not get flooded with emotion and react poorly to them because, first off, you know it isn't true. And, second of all, it's not a topic you have emotion linked to. But when your partner says "hey, it would have been nice of you to help with the dishes instead of watch TV," for what feels like the tenth time, you definitely have an emotion linked to it coming from a person that does matter to you and who you don't want to disappoint. Your emotion has been stored right alongside that conversation, phrase, word, tone of voice, or facial expression from your partner. That is what creates it as an actual memory in your mind.

Memories get stored when you have an image/experience that is linked with an emotion. When some event in your relationship reminds you of that image/experience, it isn't just the image that comes back into your mind, but also the emotion that was linked to it. Hence the term emotional trigger. Some event reminded you of something that happened in the past and triggered it to come back to the forefront of your mind and elicit the same exact emotional feeling you had when it first happened. It's almost like you are actually living it again! To make things even trickier, you might not even be aware that you're reliving an experience from the past and you're convinced that it's because of what's happening right now—that leads to you blaming it on the outside circumstance or your partner. Oftentimes your triggers feel like a real outside attack. You may be convinced that what is being said or done is a real threat to you, and you have to react back.

These memories can also stem from events outside of your current relationship, like a past relationship, events with your parents, or friends in your teen years. Without awareness, these unresolved experiences have the power to wreak havoc on your relationship. We'll share two examples.

The first example is related to triggers in friendships (which can also happen). Just a year ago, Jocelyn was at a group weekend event all centered around getting supportive ideas to help entrepreneurs grow their businesses. There were about 50 people with her in Los Angeles in the hotel conference room, and most of the attendees had worked with each other before. On the second morning, she suddenly felt flooded with resentment, outrage, and a feeling of being alone. It came on so suddenly and strongly that she didn't feel like herself, so she went to the bathroom to collect her thoughts. All she could see in her mind were the other women in the group talking amongst themselves, and not coming up to Jocelyn to talk as much. She could think of example after example of how this particular group of women made her feel like they were in the "cool club," and she was on the outside. She started to see them as the mean girls. Everything in her wanted to unfriend them on Facebook, ignore them in the room, and part of her wanted to even gossip about them being a mean group of women. It really felt real for her.

Without awareness, this scenario would have led Jocelyn to completely retreat from the group, feeling worthless and rejected. She was on the verge of deciding to stop talking to anyone, and just try to get through the weekend. Thankfully, she had the awareness of what her triggers are, how to catch them in the moment, and process through each of the three parts of a trigger (that we'll describe below). She realized that what was actually getting triggered were past memories of not feeling cool in high school and always comparing herself to that cool club that hung out together all the time. She lived for years feeling like she wasn't in that crowd and that created insecurities inside of her. It was the same insecurities that were getting triggered by how she perceived the other women acting at the conference, when in reality, they had just known each other a lot longer and had closer bonds.

Without identifying it as a personal trigger, Jocelyn would have seen the problem as *them*, and that they were at fault for how she felt. On the other hand, by identifying it as a personal trigger, she could take control by looking inside of herself and saying, "Jocelyn, this is about *you*, not them." So, you could think of a trigger as an unresolved sensitivity. It's that hidden button inside of you that comes from a past experience that didn't feel good, or you didn't fully process. That's why you'll hear people say "you're pushing my buttons." But, that saying is pointing the finger at someone else, rather than you actually looking at why or what is being pushed (or squeezed, if you went back to the orange analogy).

For some couples, these emotional triggers are like a blind spot in a poorly designed car; they're hidden from their view. It can cause people to think the best solution is to leave the relationship. But you know what you take to the next relationship? You, and your same triggers. Sure, sometimes your triggers originate in your current romantic relationship, which is why your partner gets the brunt of your reaction. But a lot of times, your emotional triggers come from something that was created much earlier on in life. This means they have been with you for quite a while.

We said we'd share another example from our own life, so here's one from Jocelyn's previous romantic relationships. In every single relationship that Jocelyn was in—whether she was sixteen or twenty-six—she experienced a great deal of jealousy. She did not trust her partners and would often ask questions like "who are you texting?", "did you talk to any girls when you were out last night?", or even harshly say "were you just looking at that girl walking by?" Her and her partner at the time would often get into massive arguments when she would yell, cry, and threaten to end the relationship. She felt insecure, and it came off as trying to control her partners or badger them with questions. At the time of these relationships, she had never heard of emotional triggers so it truly felt like her partners were the ones to blame. She thought *if only they were more honest, if only they didn't keep things from me, if only they didn't look at girls.* To her, it was always that they were not trustworthy. She'd end that relationship thinking that the next partner would be more worthy of her trust. But what did she carry into the next relationship? Her insecurity, lack of trust, and her particular triggering events (that we'll describe below).

When she started her self-development journey, Jocelyn took an honest look at the patterns in her romantic relationships. Specifically, she focused on what triggered her and where they came from in her past. In her reflections she realized that it stemmed from her first boyfriend cheating on her, and someone in her close family cheating on their own partner, which then ended in an intense divorce. While growing up, she didn't realize that those two events created such a strong belief that influenced how she related to men in general—that they are cheaters. Which could have easily continued into all her future relationships.

But she decided not to let those events be triggers any longer by using the tools below. Because of these tools, and putting them into practice, she is proud to say that she had zero jealousy starting her relationship with me (Aaron). She never feels threatened if I'm talking to a female at a workshop or event, she doesn't constantly monitor and ask what I'm looking at, and she doesn't worry about who I'm texting with. It's evident that we have cultivated trust in our relationship through setting specific agreements, actions, and promises to each other. But the point is, this triumph came from Jocelyn looking at the triggers inside of herself, not from trying to change me. As a reminder for you, any emotion that gets triggered is not because someone else did something to you, but because that emotion was already living within you and stored as a memory. This is your internal orange juice!

THE THREE PARTS OF AN EMOTIONAL TRIGGER

Now that you know your emotional triggers are inside of you, let's go into detail about the three parts that make up an emotional trigger. Once you know these, you will be able to notice when they are happening and what you can do differently.

1. The triggering event
2. The emotion that gets triggered
3. The triggered behavior

The Triggering Event

The triggering event is the outside thing that stimulates the emotion inside of you. To someone else, the thing happening could seem like no big deal, but to you it has significance and meaning. The triggering event could fall into one of these types:

1. The words being said
2. The attitude or tone of voice
3. A facial expression or body language
4. The action that was taken or not taken

The triggering event (aka the actual thing stimulating something inside of you) is not inherently a threat or attack against you, but it feels like it. The main reason that it's a trigger for you, and might not be for your friend next to you, is because it has that meaning from a past experience. Let's share some examples of "triggering events" for you:

Your partner says, "you're just like your mother." Now, for some people that would be a complete compliment and they'd say "wow, thank you so much!" But if you deep down have a fear of being like your mother because you saw traits that you didn't want to exude, this can be a triggering event for you.

Many great examples of triggering events are seen in movies. Maybe you've seen the movie *The Break-Up* with Vince Vaughn and Jennifer Aniston that's based on a relationship going downhill quickly. If you haven't seen it, this will only be a slight spoiler alert. There's a scene that takes place in their kitchen after they both get done with work, and right before they're about to have people over for dinner. She asked him to bring home 12 lemons for her table centerpiece, but he brought home only three of them. He was sitting down to relax and watch TV when she became very frustrated that he didn't do exactly what she asked. They end up having a heated discussion where she was especially upset about it, and it became one of the main upsets leading to the end of their relationship. But why? Was it about the lemons? No, it wasn't about the lemons! It was a triggering event for her because it meant that he didn't listen, was not putting in the effort, and that he took her for granted. To anyone else, some missing lemons wouldn't necessarily have that level of significance, meaning a triggering event is specific to you because of what it means to you. We'll share one more quick story before we go into the four types of triggering events.

When we first purchased our house, it needed a few things fixed up, including the dishwasher. Aaron decided to take on the task of learning how to install a new one without any outside help. After he completed it successfully, he was about as excited as a kid on Christmas morning! A few days later he started to notice that I (Jocelyn) was loading the dishes in a disorganized way: putting heavy bowls on top and randomly stacking the plates and cups. Aaron didn't say anything for a few days, but he eventually became very frustrated and said harshly, "do you really have to keep putting the heavy bowls on the top rack and just throwing the dishes in randomly? I keep having to reload them!"

Now, I was quite surprised by his reaction because, to me, the dishwasher really was not a big deal. But Aaron wasn't upset because he really cared all that much about dishes, he was upset because I wasn't acknowledging or respecting the work that he had put in to replace the dishwasher. It was as if I didn't care at all about the effort that he put in. So, jot this down . . .

> You're never upset for the reason you think you are. It's never about the dishes! It's never about the socks on the ground! It's not because they came home late from work! *It's because of what those things mean to you.*

There is still more to uncover about triggered events that take you down the path to having an Argument Hangover, so let's get into each type of triggering event in more detail. It's important that you discover what specifically triggers you and your partner so that you can shorten your Argument Hangovers together. You'll likely find that your triggers will be different from each other, and that they can change over your lifetime.

Triggering Event #1: The Words Being Said
As we said earlier, different words or phrases can trigger emotion in you. These may not be the same words that trigger your partner. We received dozens of submissions from our community when we asked what statements made by their partner trigger them, and here are just a few examples:

- "It doesn't matter/we'll figure it out later."
- "You should . . ."
- "Everyone knows you don't say/do that."

- "When are you going to . . . ?"
- "I know you're sensitive because of your past about _____."
- "You never _____."
- "Calm down."
- "I can't believe we're having this conversation."

It is our belief that words are the most common type of triggering event. If you heard any of the above words out of context, they probably wouldn't be all that threatening. But when the words feel like they have significance, especially coming from your partner, they are a trigger for you. It would be powerful for you to reflect on why these particular words trigger you. What is it about these words? Is it linked to a specific memory or person from your past? Do you feel that what they are saying means something is wrong or not good enough about you?

For example, take the words "I need my space." If you really just read it plainly, it's not that scary. But you could interpret these words to mean "I need space from *you*" or "I am disappointed in you, so I need to be away from you" or "I am not enjoying being around you right now." If you can identify why certain phrases hit a sensitive spot inside of you, you have more power in not letting them control you.

We want to address one particular phrase that uses absolutes because those frequently show up when we ask what triggers people. Using an absolute is when you say "you always" or "you never" to your partner. It very frequently is listed as a trigger by men in particular. Here's why: the defending partner thinks, "that's not true, I don't always _____." It's a very blanket statement to make that your partner 100 percent of the time did or did not do something. For the logical and left-brain partners, it's easy to have a defense and prove that it's not true. Now your partner is in a place to prove you wrong. When what you really meant by using an absolute was that in your experience, this event has happened often. This pits you against each other because one is trying to convey their emotional experience with words, while the other is trying to logically defend their position by "discrediting" the other person.

A powerful exercise for you before moving on to the second type of triggering event is to write down the exact words that trigger you, and what those words means to you. Remember, it's the meaning behind the words that are causing it to be a trigger event that elicits your emotions.

What's being said (the words/phrase):	What it means to you:	*Why* it has that meaning:
"Never mind."	"They don't care enough to keep talking about this."	It reminds you of a past relationship where your partner completely gave up.
"What did you do today?"	"They don't think that me taking care of the kids is productive enough."	You fear that being a stay-at-home parent isn't seen as big of a contribution as going to work.
"Why did you do it that way?"	"They think the way you did it makes no sense, and you should have done it their way."	It reminds you of your dad telling you that you did something wrong and you hated disappointing him.
Write down your examples:	*Write down your examples:*	*Write down your examples:*

Triggering Event #2: The Attitude or Tone of Voice

For some, the tone of voice used by your partner can be more of a triggering event than the words being used. The same sentence could be said with two different attitudes/tones of voice and it would impact you differently. Your partner could say "can you help with the dishes" calmly and it wouldn't bother you, but if said at a higher volume, with an air of frustration, it could trigger bad feelings.

When we go deeper into conversation with our clients, they often realize that their partner's tone of voice reminds them of feeling punished or talked down to. Joe in our community said it perfectly when he said "sometimes there's a hint of being talked down to, especially if what I'm doing isn't like how she would handle it. My mother does that." You might feel that way as well if it reminds you of how one of your parents talked to you, or maybe a rude kid in school that bullied you. Of course, your partner would ideally want to work on having a more loving tone of voice, but it's important for you to identify why you react to it. If you knew that it was one of your triggering events, you could calmly say to them "hey, let's please talk more lovingly to each other" as a reminder to your partner, rather than barking back.

You also could have a reaction if your partner's attitude or tone of voice feels shut down to you. For example, your partner might be more reserved and when you ask them if they're okay and they say, "yeah, I'm fine" in a more solemn way, you might start to feel that it is a triggering event. We'll talk more about your different communication personality types on page 151, but note here if you get triggered when your partner's attitude appears more withdrawn. It might be in those moments when they say they are fine, but their tone of voice and overall attitude reminds you of people who shut you out.

Triggering Event #3: A Facial Expression or Body Language

You can likely already envision a particular expression on your partner's face when they start to get annoyed or frustrated. They probably have a certain look with their eyes or eyebrows, a way their mouth curls up, or even the tenseness of the muscles in their face that tell you all too well what they are feeling or thinking, right? It's pretty funny how many of us are able to interpret our partner's every little quirk or movement.

If you think about it, it's really just the facial muscles moving in a bizarre way, which isn't inherently threatening. In fact, they could just as likely be constipated and making a sour face from how they feel. But when it's directed at you, their face means a great deal more and can stir up different emotions. Maybe it reminds you of your parents when they were disappointed in you as a kid. The last thing you ever wanted to see was your mom or dad disappointed in you. Maybe an ex looked at you a certain way, right before having a conversation about ending the relationship. See, it's not necessarily your partner's facial expression that is triggering you (because it's just facial muscles moving), it's what it reminds you of and what it means to you in that moment.

Or, most commonly, your partner's facial expression automatically reminds you of how things have gone before. You think *oh, here's this again, I know exactly what's going to happen* or *okay, they're upset again, what did I do now?* You've mentally stored these negative interpretations from previous interactions and use it as ammo or justification for assuming you know the meaning behind your partner's every move. This only leads you down the path of making false assumptions about your partner that will only swiftly carry you right into these emotional triggering events. Reflect for a moment if certain facial expressions or body language reminds you of something from your upbringing, or of how difficult conversations tend to go with your partner.

Triggering Event #4: An Action (Taken or Not Taken)
This last type of triggering event involves an action taken, or sometimes even more hurtful, an action not taken. Let's say your partner went out with coworkers after a day of work, did not tell you, and didn't return home until late at night. Even if they did not intend to

cause an upset, you could be triggered with feelings of being disrespected or that they keep things from you.

To depict how not taking action can also be a trigger, we'll share a brief story from a couple we worked with. They almost felt embarrassed to talk about the events that triggered their arguments because logically they knew it wasn't a "big" deal, even though it caused big fights. It had to do with taking out the trash. She was very frustrated that he would claim he'd help with the trash, but then didn't take it out for two or three days after it was already full. He made statements like, "it's just the trash, it's not that big of a deal," which would only make her feel more frustrated and resentful. What we helped them discover together was that the trash itself wasn't the big deal, but it's what it meant to each of them. She had a big aha moment when she realized that him not taking out the trash brought up concerns about starting to have children together. She had an unconscious fear that if he was going to slack on taking out the trash, he might not be a team player in waking up for their crying child, or changing diapers, or even eventually helping them with homework. Recognizing this was really helpful for him to understand the bigger picture of why it upset her so much when he wasn't taking care of the trash. He no longer dismissed her remarks about it, and started taking actions to help her feel overall like he's a team player. Now, a couple years later, they are happily raising children and loving it.

Hopefully what you take away from this example is that it's not about whether you think the actions/non-action matter to you or whether they seem "worth" getting so upset about. It's about what those actions/non-actions really mean to you or your partner. Go beyond looking at the mechanics of the action, and look for the more important message it conveys.

Here are some additional examples of actions/non-actions that our clients were triggered by, and why, that you may relate to in your own relationship.

- He was coming home from work later and missing family dinners. (This triggered the feeling of not being prioritized and that her partner didn't want to spend time with her.)
- She didn't plan anything special for his birthday. (This triggered in him a feeling of not being appreciated.)
- He wasn't initiating sexual intimacy as often. (This triggered in her feelings of insecurity about her body and fear that he didn't desire her anymore.)
- She was spending more money than they agreed upon. (This triggered feelings in him of not being respected and being undermined.)
- He looked at another woman fondly. (This triggered past feelings of being cheated on.)

Spend a minute reflecting on what actions/non-actions are triggering events for you, but also ask yourself *why*. What does that actually mean to you? Here is a prompt to get you thinking about it:

When my partner does/does not _____, it means to me that _____
_____. It likely is a triggering event to me because _____ happened in the past.

It is powerful to understand what your trigger points are, because you will be able to keep emotion from escalating as fast and shorten your time being disconnected from or mad at your partner. We do have a warning, however. Do not set the expectation that you will be able to get rid of all your triggers, because they will change during your life together, and you will form new ones. The point here is to realize when a trigger event is happening, whether for you or for your partner, and in those moments to be aware of what your reaction is. Imagine what it would be like to have a partnership in which you didn't react to each other's triggering events, but supported each other in identifying and healing them.

The Emotion that Gets Triggered

Hopefully you already had a couple of aha moments in this chapter, and we've only gotten through the first of the three parts of emotional triggers. Let's go back now to the main topic of emotional triggers to remember that they really are linked to memory. When you or your partner activate one of these event triggers you just identified, it brings up stored emotion. Can you feel what the emotion is when that event happened? How do you feel? Do you feel sad, upset, angry? Do you start to get defensive? This is the second part of an emotional trigger. It's the actual emotion that gets triggered.

In the moments that you're triggered, it's critical that you learn to more clearly label the feeling. Don't generalize it by just saying "I'm mad" or "I'm hurt." Especially when your true feeling isn't just "mad." That's really just a defense mechanism for something more vulnerable that you're feeling. Labeling the feeling gives you more self-awareness and allows you to take responsibility for your emotions and corresponding actions. It also benefits your partner because they can learn more about you and understand where you are coming from. Like we said, true intimacy is "in-to-me-you-see." And that includes even the not-so-fun emotions. It may seem counterintuitive but you actually get to know your partner on a deeper level when you understand more of what causes them pain and not just pleasure. When you label your emotions, it gives your partner the opportunity to empathize with you. As former lead FBI negotiator Chris Voss writes in his book *Never Split the Difference,* a negotiation can start to move toward a resolution once you empathize with the other person.[1] This happens when you can specifically label the emotion they are feeling. So, how do you go about this?

---

1   Voss, Chris. *Never Split the Difference*. New York: Harper Business, 2016.

The book *Emotional Intelligence* points to the five main categories of emotion: happy, sad, angry, afraid, and ashamed.[2] But within those categories are more specific words you could use to identify the degree to which you're experiencing that emotion.

Happy could be: excited, elated, passionate, relieved, satisfied, content, pleased, etc.

Sad could be: alone, hurt, hopeless, lost, distressed, disappointed, or dissatisfied.

Angry could be: furious, outraged, betrayed, frustrated, disgusted, irritated, or touchy.

Afraid could be: shocked, panicky, threatened, insecure, worried, or unsure.

Ashamed could be: remorseful, dishonored, unworthy, guilty, regretful, or silly.

Do you see how each of the five main categories encompasses varying degrees of emotion? It's so important to learn to identify these as you work through your triggers. Once you can identify and accurately label your emotion, you can start to shift your language during your arguments to go from vague to more specific and productive.

Instead of saying this (being vague, and passing blame):	Say something like this (labeling the feeling and identifying the trigger):
I am so pissed at you, _____ (their name).	I am feeling frustrated because this is triggering some unresolved feelings I have.
I am so mad at you, _____ (their name).	This is triggering old feelings of betrayal from times that _____ (where it came from).
I am hurt because you _____.	I'm feeling disrespected because this triggered the past memory of _____.

---

2 Goleman, Daniel. *Emotional Intelligence*. New York: Bantam, 2005.

If you're reading those prompts and doubting that you two could ever talk that way with each other, remember that this all takes practice. It's going to take time to become more self-aware of your emotions and share them calmly from a place of taking ownership of them (instead of pointing the finger at them). It's also going to take practice for your partner to listen to you talk about your emotions from a non-defensive place. But imagine after consistently practicing this step, you can share the emotions getting triggered and your partner says, "I totally hear you, tell me more about that!" Wouldn't that in itself shorten your Argument Hangover?

The Triggered Behavior

The third and final part of an emotional trigger is the triggered behavior. The triggered behavior is what you tend to do as you're feeling a particular emotion. It's usually an unconscious reaction. When a triggering event happens and you feel emotion starting to flood your body, it typically triggers an automatic behavioral pattern.

Think of this for a moment like when a movie character has an eruption of emotion. You probably think to yourself *I know what they are about to do.* This is the same thing that happens to you! If you could only watch yourself like you were in a movie, you would know exactly what was going to happen next. Anyone that would be watching you could see what you were going to do next (if only you could see yourself that way)! When triggered, you have a default and predictable reaction to your partner, which often leads to more damage than the original cause of the argument. This is what really extends the Argument Hangover period.

To have this book be truly impactful and to reduce the time spent in the Argument Hangover (to keep the conflict from doing even more damage to the relationship), you will need to pinpoint what your default behavior is. We'd like you to connect the triggering event and the labeled emotion you filled in the table on page 62 to what you normally do next. Is it something that you immediately say? "No, that's not true. Why do you always say that? You're the one that started this conversation. You're the one that always brings this up. This is your fault!" Maybe you tense up, leave the room, or maybe leave the house and go for a drive. Maybe you yell, maybe your voice and tone rises. What is it for you?

Triggering Event (fill in from table on pg. 62)	Triggered Emotion (fill in from table on pg. 62)	Triggered Behavior (what do you automatically do next?)

Your predictable triggered behaviors come from a triggering event and resulting emotion that follows it. Behaviors that happen consistently over time take a conflict (which could just be contrasting views that you have) and push you into the Argument Hangover. The Argument Hangover gets worse because of this automatic behavior, which can cause more damage to your relationship. Your actions right in this moment hurt your connection as well as the safety and trust you have with each other if you allow yourself to make it even more personal and attack your partner because of a misguided idea that you have to defend yourself to survive.

If you love the science behind behavioral patterns, this next section is for you! What is actually happening in these moments is what is referred to as an "amygdala hijack." Normally your brain takes in the signals from your senses, then processes and analyzes these inputs before deciding what bodily functions to activate down through the central nervous system (CNS). But there is a part of your brain, the amygdala, that is responsible for the fight, flight, or freeze responses when you are in perceived danger. This is great if you are walking down the street and about to get hit by a bus you didn't see, because this allows you to jump out of the way without having to "think about it." But if you get emotionally triggered by talking to your partner, it causes the same type of automatic (and typically hurtful) response as the amygdala hijack activates an automatic program (which is effectively this triggered behavior). Again, this does not happen because your partner causes you to feel this way. It's because your emotional trigger cycle was already there within you. Your pattern of behavior is what gets you into battle against your partner. This is where your arguments turn into a free-for-all, like a boxing match with no rules, that do real damage to the connection with your partner.

In your own mind you are justified to swear. You may bring up the past, compare your partner to a prior relationship or the negative characteristics of their parents. You may even bring up past hurts that you never brought up before as ammo to cut them down in return. Let's be real here; you know exactly what we're talking about. There is something that you may not have shared before because you didn't want to rock the boat or cause an argument, so you've been holding it inside. You've been feeling upset and wishing they hadn't said it that way. You wish they hadn't brought up that past circumstance again, but you didn't allow yourself to be vulnerable and honest enough to say it. This can create an emotional trigger within you that could last for days, weeks, months, or longer if not addressed.

Up to this point the triggered behavior has been an outward action. Yet we do not want to step over the fact that a triggered behavior can also include shutting down and isolating yourself from your partner. It's this aspect that is largely misunderstood. If you fall into this camp (like Aaron in the beginning) even though you think it's a good idea to hold an emotion in and not react at all, it can be just as harmful. Yes, in the short-term you may avoid an argument, but in the long-run you are setting yourself up for creating more emotional triggers, more opportunity to prolong and escalate the Argument Hangover. The more you hold an emotion in (just like the soda bottle that builds up pressure when it is shaken), the more resentment will build toward your partner. However, you have already started to shift your perspective on what a conflict really is from the first few chapters, so you're more ready to embrace it!

HOW EMOTIONAL TRIGGERS IMPACT THE ARGUMENT HANGOVER

When you continue to build up this emotional trigger inside of you, one day it will all blow up! If you're not aware of how the three parts of an emotional trigger show up in your relationship, you may unconsciously cause more damage than the original cause of the disagreement. Your behavior can become destructive and, in some ways, violent, meaning you criticize, blame, have a sharp tone, say hurtful things, isolate, or shut down. These all cause more damage than the original conflict, right? You may even irrationally justify physical abuse and violence against your own partner (which, by the way, is *never* acceptable).

Whether you fall on the side of shutting down or outwardly expressing your emotion when you're triggered, you have the opportunity to become more aware of your triggered action. The fact is, the harsher, the more extreme, and the more emotion present when triggered, the longer the Argument Hangover will last. Maybe it'll only be a day or two before you come back and say that you are sorry or forgive each other, but when you raise this level of emotional trigger within the heat of the argument, it becomes even more devastating later. You may continue to harbor resentment and anger for how far your partner was willing to take the conflict.

This is a good moment to pause and reflect on how far you have come in this chapter with the goal of keeping your emotional triggers from escalating and prolonging the Argument Hangover period. You may have already noticed what the triggered event might be for you, what the emotion is that gets triggered, and what your behavior is that follows. What is the pattern that automatically happens for you? Is it an automatic verbal response? Is it an automatic movement of your body or your own facial expressions? Or do you just up and leave the room? What is your "favorite flavor," as we like to say, for when emotion gets triggered? What is it that you predictably do? Are you ready to keep emotional triggers from happening over and over, and from prolonging your Argument Hangover? Sure, you are! So, let's dive into how to have more power when you are triggered.

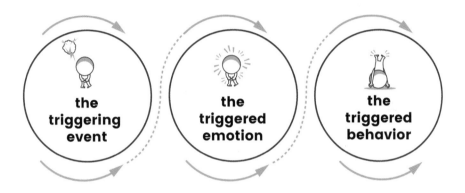

the
triggering
event

the
triggered
emotion

the
triggered
behavior

USE PATTERN INTERRUPTS

You are more powerful than your triggers! You have the ability to take ownership of them and interrupt the cycle before they cause more harm. How? This process of interrupting is one that has been made more widely known (and you could say famous for those of us that spend all of our time in the personal development and performance world) by Tony Robbins. You yourself may have pursued personal development or overall performance in your own life, so you probably have come across Tony Robbins talks about "Pattern Interrupts."

You may be asking yourself *well, now that I notice these emotional triggers and my patterns of behavior, what can I actually do about them?* (This, by the way, is the exact question you should be asking yourself!) The next step then is to start incorporating a pattern interrupt into the conflicts with your partner. What this means is that you have to put something in place that breaks the cycle and keeps you from automatically (and by default) going into your triggered behavior. One way to incorporate a pattern interrupt is by a body movement or a phrase that is so far outside of the programming that it causes your subconscious mind to stop running that program. From your mind's perspective it's like a jolt that says "oh wait, this must not be the same event I'm used to, because something different happened." Once this happens you are able to get back into the conscious mind and become more aware of what is actually happening, what you are really saying, and who you are talking to. You're back in a place where you actually decide what it is you want to do next rather than be run by that previous program.

What a pattern interrupt might actually look like is a word that has nothing to do with what you're talking about. We like to use a "code word" like marshmallow or blueberries that is so obscure that it causes us to actually pause and say "wait a minute, we notice we are about to go down a path that is not going to serve us or our relationship." This is the very first goal to breaking the emotional trigger cycle. This is also a good way to bring in some humor to interrupt your typical behavior and argument patterns to keep you from getting into the Argument Hangover period. And guess what? Using humor is a great way to break your argument pattern because you both can actually smile and change the state and your attitude toward each other.

Before you go out there and try this with your partner, what you have to do with this humorous code word is first agree to use it. Before either one of you can use a particular word like blueberries, marshmallow, or any other type of obscure word you choose, you must both agree that it can be used and you both know the intent. Otherwise if you choose something random to say for yourself when you get into these argument patterns, then your partner might feel like you're not taking it seriously. It might seem like you are trying to brush it off which can cause your partner to be even more defensive.

However, if you agree ahead of time, then when one of you uses it, the other partner will quickly remember "oh yeah, we've agreed to this and it reminds me that we're going to stop this pattern before it takes us any further into the Argument Hangover."

We realize that being funny might not fit for everyone, so there is another way to do this, rather than have it be humorous. You can use a word or a phrase to remind you that you are actually on the same side. Our favorite phrase is "same team." When we use the phrase "same team," this accomplishes the same result as a pattern interrupt. It snaps us out of the subconscious defensive pattern we were about to go into, and reminds us in milliseconds that we might be feeling a lot of emotion, we may have triggered this event within each other, and we're starting to go into this predictable pattern, but we really are on the same team here. We don't need to be against each other, so let's pause, come together, and seek to connect. Let's remind each other that we can face this challenge together. Even though we might have opposing views, let's remember that this can actually be a benefit for us. This can be something that clarifies a new desire, a new want, a new expression that we'd like to share with each other to ultimately become even more connected. (We realize that a lot was just said in our own minds, almost an entire paragraph, within just a millisecond; but all of these words are really to try and describe the immediate feeling we have with each other. All by just saying "same team.")

USE EMOTIONAL OUTLETS

If you don't implement emotional outlets into your life, your triggers will keep running the show. Imagine a soda bottle. When you shake the bottle over and over, what happens? Pressure starts to build up within it, doesn't it? And if you keep on shaking that bottle, what's eventually going to happen? Well, the pressure is going to build up so much that it's going to explode. This is such an accurate analogy to what happens when you have emotion that continues to get stored up within your body and doesn't get released.

We live in such a fast-paced world that it can be hard to prioritize your mental and emotional health. Both you and your partner have many different pressures on you, and you might carry those into your home and your relationship. Whether it's your job, your kids, your health, or something with your family, if you don't have an emotional outlet, your tolerance threshold is much lower. Said another way, you have a short fuse, and are much more prone to getting triggered. But at the end of the day, your to-do list is not as important as your emotional health. We've heard countless partners say "I don't care about having a clean kitchen if it means you're stressed out and short with me all the time." Your partner would rather be around someone who is taking care of themselves, therefore communicating well, and not quick to start up a fight because of having a short fuse.

The other important aspect of having emotional outlets is that you release the frustrations and conflicts that come up in your relationship. Don't suppress your feelings or they are much more likely to get triggered again. Even after you two resolve things, it's important to release any sadness, anger, or fear, otherwise it will be there waiting for you the next time something reminds you of that. An emotional outlet (back to the soda bottle analogy) is similar to unscrewing the top of the bottle to let some of the pressure out rather than continuing to allow the pressure to build up until it explodes. If you actually wanted to drink out of the bottle after it had already been shaken, you would open the cap a little bit to let some of the pressure out and repeat until all the pressure dissipated. Well, this is what you want to do with emotion you are building up within yourself. Healthy emotional outlets can look like:

- Self-soothing: journaling, exercise, and letting yourself cry and release
- Talking with a trusted confidant or expert
- Sharing with your partner, if you two can listen non-reactively

For the first emotional outlet, self-soothing, exercise is extremely powerful. Go on a run and let out the emotion, take a boxing class, go to yoga to calm your nervous system. Try different things to discover what helps you move that emotion. Think about this, emotion is just "energy in motion." That's why you have to move that e-motion out in a healthy way. You could also try journaling and letting yourself reflect and release what is coming up for you. Don't write off journaling without trying it; it can be very healing.

The second emotional outlet, a trusted confidant, could be a trusted friend or family member or coach. Note that this is not "gossiping" to someone, and it's important that you and your partner both agree that it's okay to share with these particular people. Gossiping sounds like "ugh, they pissed me off again because they _____," whereas sharing for the sake of an emotional outlet is "I've had some feelings of sadness come up for me because I'm being reminded of old feelings of not being good enough." Notice the big difference between the two? It may best suit you to seek out an expert who has studied and trained in emotional release exercises or processing emotions, or a skilled relationship coach. Don't wait until "something is wrong" to work with an expert, do that proactively.

Regardless of which emotional outlet you pick (or try a combo), it is important to use at least one. Emotion is energy in motion so it must find a way to move. Otherwise you will continue to store it in your body and turn into the emotional trigger that escalates and prolongs your Argument Hangover period!

YOUR GAME PLAN

The big takeaway from this chapter is how emotional triggers can instigate and escalate conflicts and prolong the Argument Hangover . . . if you don't have awareness of them. But if you're aware of them, you are able to interrupt them so that your conversations are more constructive, and you can ideally avoid the Argument Hangover altogether. With that awareness you can also set yourself up to have an emotional outlet to reduce the internal pressure of stored up emotions and further reduce the chance of hangovers in the future.

- What are three of your triggering events?
- What is the specific emotion you then feel and where in your body do you feel it?
- What is your corresponding automatic behavior that happens next?
- What type of emotional outlet will be best for you to set up right now?
- Share your responses with each other, and come up with ways to remember what your partner's triggers are so you have more context for when they come up.

Here is one last inspirational and aspirational point of view once you have worked through the game plan steps. What was covered in this chapter were the events, emotions, and behaviors that lead to negative reactions toward your partner. Now, think of the flip side. What if all of your emotional triggers were positive responses? What if you reverse engineered this emotional triggering process so that no matter what event or circumstance came up for the rest of your life, the emotion that came up was encouragement, curiosity, intrigue, or excitement? What if from those emotions you automatically acted for the benefit of you and your relationship? Wouldn't that be amazing and extraordinary? You would live your life with your partner as a true empowered couple that could create anything you desired for your life together with speed, clarity, and joy! Said another way, what if you cultivated a relationship where you saw triggers as revealing a gift that only benefited your partnership? What a partnership you would have that would certainly leave a legacy for all those that got to interact with you during your life. This is an aspirational goal of course, but just as the emotional trigger sequence works in one direction, it can work in the other!

You can shorten the Argument Hangover by recognizing and managing your personal emotional triggers.

5

BEFORE CONFLICT

"When you fail to plan, you plan to fail."

—Benjamin Franklin

This opening quote isn't normally associated with marriage, but it couldn't be more relevant. Unfortunately, most couples don't really come up with a pre-plan for how they'll handle conflict. When you first started dating each other, you likely didn't sit down and say "so babe, how do we want to fight? What are our ground rules?" No, the questions asked (albeit still important) are: what do you like to do for fun? What is your favorite movie? What are your career goals?

We have talked with hundreds of couples who are investing $20,000 to $30,000 (some even as much as six figures) into a wedding and when we ask "what's your game plan for arguments?" they have a blank stare on their faces. They know what flowers they want for the ceremony and even have a spreadsheet for their wedding details, but they lack a written game plan for the most critical things . . . like how to handle conflict! Don't worry, you're not alone if you didn't talk about fighting while dating. It's our intent that talking about "how you'll fight" will eventually become a norm in modern dating. Even if your bond was established because of your compatibility (the likes and dislikes you have in common) and chemistry (your feeling of attraction), that doesn't mean you will be healthy fight-ers. Many couples bank on the fact that they "love" each other and expect that to be enough for when the tough moments arise. But we have to share a cold-hard truth with you: love is not enough. Love is required for a great relationship, but it's not enough to overcome poor habits. "Love is what brought you together, but it's your habits that keep you together."

Of course it's important if you ask each other things like, "what's your favorite movie?" and "what are some of your career goals?" But imagine just how much more on the same page you would be if you asked questions like:

- Will you raise your voice or just leave the house when we have a fight?
- What would be our plan for times we disagree?
- What are we going to do if we have seasons of being disconnected?

While those aren't sexy or fun conversations, they're critical to having a great relationship. The fact that you both like long walks on the beach won't matter when you both are emotionally triggered and have massively different opinions on something. While you might have had some reflective conversations after big conflicts, this chapter is about how you can be even more proactive in your conflict "game plan." An NBA team doesn't decide on what offensive and defensive plays they will run after the season is over, right? So why would you wait to create a plan to defend your relationship against toxic conflict *after* it's too late?

Regardless of whether you've ever talked about how you'll handle conflict, this chapter will guide you in the right direction. In fact, in our study with the 78 couples taking the relationship assessment mentioned on page 6, on a scale of 1 to 5 from strongly disagree to strongly agree, the majority of couples selected [4 = agree] to the statement: "my partner and I have different ideas for how to solve disagreements." This shows that you aren't alone if you feel that you don't have a solid game plan for times of conflict in your relationship. It's never too late to implement these new skills, even if you're years into the relationship and worry that you've had too many tough moments. Now is the time to implement new tools in your relationship! Get ready to feel armed and empowered with pre-conflict strategies. Let's dive in.

IT'S A FREE-FOR-ALL FIGHT

Can you imagine how any professional sport would go if there weren't set ground rules? Literally imagine for a second how dangerous football or boxing would be if there weren't clear boundaries for what a "foul" or "penalty" was. That would not be a pretty sight and, frankly, it would be dangerous for the participants.

Before discovering the strategy in this section for healthy conflict, we will be honest in saying that Jocelyn was a gnarly "fighter" in past relationships. She'd be the first to admit that when her emotions were triggered, it was a free-for-all. If she was mad, she'd allow herself to yell, curse, and storm out of the room, only to come back pained with regret and remorse, begging for forgiveness out of hope of not being abandoned. That might make for good reality TV, but it doesn't work for a healthy, lasting relationship.

In the last chapter, we talked about emotional triggers and how to interrupt them. But if you don't identify them and instead let yourself go to your default "trigger behaviors," then you'll just get into a free-for-all cycle that leads to a vicious Argument Hangover. At this point, you might be recalling moments when you let yourselves have a free-for-all fight and how painful it felt afterward. Don't worry, a solution for you is coming soon.

Last May we hosted one of our couples workshops in Arizona, and a couple showed up looking like they hadn't slept the night before. She had tears in her eyes that she was trying to hold back, and he looked stone-cold mad with his arms crossed. Of course, they did their best to blend in and say hi to a few couples around them, but you could tell they were feeling the pain of an unresolved conflict that occurred in the last twenty-four hours. On the lunch break we went to spend some two-on-two time with them since we could tell they needed some additional support. After asking them a few questions, we uncovered what the trigger and content of the conflict was, but the issue we spent most of the time discussing with them was how their "free-for-all" fight was what amplified their pain. If you were watching their argument like a movie, you would have seen:

Carter: Abruptly brings up their finances and his frustration that she spends too much on things that don't seem important to him.

Taylor: Feels emotionally triggered and quickly says back "Oh, like you're so great with money, huh?! Last week you bought some crap for your man cave to play games and you tried to hide it from me."

Carter: With a raised voice, says "That's not true! I didn't hide that from you. I just took the package downstairs!"

Taylor: Lashes back, saying "That's b.s. You're just lying."

Carter: Yells, "You always do this! You turn it around on me when you're the one that's guilty of spending extra money. You're being just like your mother. Didn't you say that you don't want to be like her, huh? Well you are!"

Taylor: "How dare you say that when you're being the a-hole and controlling me."

Then they both stomp their feet out of the room and slam a different door to get space.

Unfortunately, the original cause of the conflict, money, wasn't being discussed as the argument progressed. Instead it turned into name calling, raising their voices, saying things that would trigger each other, and then leaving the room. There wasn't even a moment to talk constructively about the original subject of the disagreement.

> Think about how many arguments don't get resolved because *why* you started to fight was overtaken *by how* you started to fight.

You likely have had those moments where you ask, "what were we arguing about in the first place?" Yeah, that is more common than you'd imagine. You get off course from being solution-oriented because your poor tactics (your triggered behaviors) end up distracting you both. We can't tell you how many times we've received phone calls from clients on vacation (in gorgeous places like Fiji and Hawaii) who felt they lost out on a potentially divine day because they had one small trigger turn into a ruthless stand-off in their hotel room. Even if you're thinking *we would never yell at each other in a*

'SUBJECT' OF THE CONFLICT IS THE SAME: MONEY

free-for-all

agreements & ground rules

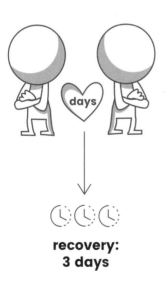

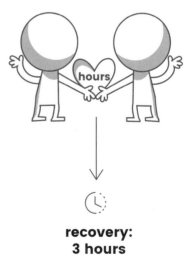

recovery: 3 days

recovery: 3 hours

hotel, it can also be painful if you two end up just sitting silently frustrated with each other while sitting on a beautiful beach. It can take the whole experience away.

The point is that you and another couple could have an argument around the same topic, but how each of you experience it, and recover from it, is determined by the way you fight: as a free-for-all or one with established agreements and ground rules. You're obviously reading this book because you're committed to implementing new tools, so let's get to the solution.

CREATING AGREEMENTS AND GROUND RULES

The first step in pre-conflict planning is to create agreements and ground rules for times of conflict. Whether you just had your very first argument or your ten-thousandth, it's time to do this activity for the sake of your relationship. Since you have started to identify many of your emotional triggers in chapter 4, you each can now take responsibility for what destructive reactions you have and come up with an agreement around it. For example, if you tend to raise your voice and slam doors when you're triggered, you definitely want to create an agreement around that.

An agreement is stating "In times of conflict, I/we will _____" or "In times of conflict, I/we will *not* _____."

It's worth noting that an agreement is not a command. You can't read this section and say to your partner "see, you're not allowed to yell at me anymore." An agreement is defined by the Oxford dictionary as "a negotiated and typically binding agreement between parties as to a course of action." Notice that it's negotiated and it's agreed upon by both people.

Agreements are extremely powerful if you truly are giving your word to what you say. Giving your word means that you are authentically and genuinely promising something. You give your energy and intention toward fulfilling that promise. As you go into the activity around creating agreements, you can't just say "Yeah, sure, I'll try." "I'll try" is just another way of saying, "I am not willing to take 100 percent responsibility or commit to doing whatever it takes to make a change." That might sound harsh, but it's true. "I'll 'try'" and "I hope I can" aren't going to cut it for a great marriage. Of course, you won't be perfect at keeping the agreements, especially if you have ingrained old patterns for years, but if you infuse the power of a true decision into your promise, it will feel like a fire of self-accountability lit inside of you. So, now that you're ready and willing to create these agreements, here's an example of what your written agreements could include:

Agreements & Ground Rules
For times of conflict

1. No swearing
2. No name calling
3. No raising your voice
4. No storming out of the room
5. No bringing up the past
6. No ultimatums
7. No interrupting
8. No slamming things
9. No shutting down and getting quiet
10. No ignoring each other
11. No important conversations via text message

It is really important that you two have your agreements written down for two reasons:

1. Science has shown that anything written down and repeated is ingrained into your subconscious mind and more likely to happen.
2. You two will be able to refer back to them and "score" yourselves as to how well you've been keeping the agreements. Without any way to measure something, how can you know if you are improving?

If you don't see an agreement listed here that is important for your relationship, make sure you mark it down and talk about it. While many of the agreements listed above seem self-explanatory as to why they're a "no-go" during an argument, there's a few we want to elaborate on.

For agreement #9, "no shutting down or getting quiet," while it's easy to think that saying nothing at all is better and less harmful than yelling or screaming, it really isn't. As discussed in the previous chapter on emotional triggers, shutting down is an unconscious default reaction to conflict for many people. This agreement is important to make so that neither of you prevent the other person from being understood. And believe it or not, shutting down is a way to control a conversation and will make your partner feel dominated.

For agreement #4, "no storming out of the room," you might wonder *but isn't it better if I get space to cool down first?* Well, it's all in your intention. To request a cooldown with the intent to change the energy is great! But storming out of the room can be a mechanism to "escape" the conversation and avoid hearing something you don't want to. We'll go into detail about a more constructive way to get space in the next chapter.

The goal of creating agreements is to build them into new habits. Just like it takes time for you to build the habit of going to the gym in the morning or to drink water instead of soda, it will take you time for your agreements to become your new habits. There will be times that you "mess up" in the beginning, and that's to be expected. A habit is formed, obviously, by repetition. While many books have declared that it takes "21 days" or "30 days" or "60 days" to form a new habit, it will likely take each of you a different amount of time to embody your new agreements. One study performed by Dr. Phillippa Lally found that among the 96 participants over 12 weeks, everyone reported the new behavior became automatic in vastly different time frames.[1] For some, it took 18 days and for others 254 days to report the new activity as a habit—that's quite a big difference, right?

Taking this information into consideration, you can expect that you and your partner will still revert back to old conflict patterns at times and that you both will implement these new agreements in slightly different time frames. A key ingredient in this will be having grace! You must have grace for yourself and for your partner when you forget to stick to the agreement. Neither of you will be perfect right from the start, so make sure to "own up" to when you don't keep an agreement, and be quick to forgive each other when you make a mistake. Focus on the fact that you are making progress, instead of perfection. Here's our recommended process for creating your agreements:

1. Block approximately 30 to 60 minutes to have this conversation together in a calm state.
2. Each of you should write down 5 to 10 agreements individually based on some of your past triggered or automatic behaviors.

---

1 Lally, Phillippa. "How habits are formed: Modelling habit formation in the real world." *European Journal of Social Psychology* 40(6) (2009):881–1094.

3. Then, compare notes and establish a combined list with the top 4 most important agreements for you together.
4. Each of you should say out loud some version of "I promise to keep these agreements, and I will own up to the times I don't keep them, as we form them into our new habits."
5. Hug and high-five . . . because you're a team!
6. Then, place your written agreements somewhere visible and review them often (weekly or monthly) to make sure they remain relevant.

You might be wondering why we suggested you focus on your top 4 agreements. This is because it will likely take focus to break your old destructive patterns, and to stick with the new agreements. If you're trying to master 10 agreements at once, you could feel overwhelmed or just not remember them at all. The first 4 agreements are the ones that will make the biggest difference now. These will be the ones that help prevent doing the most harm to each other in times of conflict, and the ones that will shorten your Argument Hangovers. Focus on those 4 now, then you can add in additional agreements later. Don't worry, later on we'll talk about what happens if/when you break an agreement. For now, let's go into the next before-conflict strategy to prevent the Argument Hangover.

CONFLICTS BECOME MORE CHALLENGING WITH LOW "LOVE ACCOUNTS"

While writing this book, we received a call from a client we have supported throughout various great seasons as well as challenging seasons in their relationship. John said to us, "We just cannot get connected. Lately the arguments have been so frequent that it's hard to get back to a place where we desire to be around each other or to be affectionate." We asked him, "On a scale of 0 to 100 percent, how full would you say your 'love bank account' is right now?"

John replied, "5 out 100 percent."

We then asked, "What do you imagine her response would be?"

John said, "Probably the same. We both feel really off."

We explained, "It's imperative to know that conflicts will feel more significant and personal when your love accounts are low. You can't fill your love account from 5 percent to 100 percent all at once either. You fill your love account in small increments that add up over time. It won't feel natural to go from feeling really hurt to all of a sudden loving and affectionate. It's rare for anyone to close that gap quickly. But it can still happen faster than it took you to get down to 5 percent in the first place."

To take this further, here's what you need to know about your "love account" and how to consistently keep it full. We greatly respect the research of Dr. Gary Chapman and John Gottman who each coined the phrases "love tank" and "emotional bank account" respectively. In our work with couples, we call this the "love account." Your love account describes an invisible, internal "bank account" gauging how loved and appreciated you feel. When your love account is drained, you can feel more insecure, discouraged, or disconnected from your partner. When your love account is full, you feel more hopeful, genuinely loved by your partner, and connected to them.

As you can imagine, a lower love account can lead to you having a shorter fuse and more difficulty in healing from an Argument Hangover. It also leads to the hangovers happening more frequently. This is the type of experience that John was having after weeks of recurring conflicts. Both of their love accounts were so low that he felt hopeless and unsure of how to come back to love and connection. But having a lower love account was also one of the root causes of their recurring conflicts. It makes you feel like you are in a downward spiral leading to more and more disconnection.

For John and Skylar, they not only were feeling the repercussions of their recurring conflicts, but also the months of being "too busy" to nurture the relationship that led to their low love accounts. Week after week, they neglected to prioritize their partnership. Which is

when the love account is low

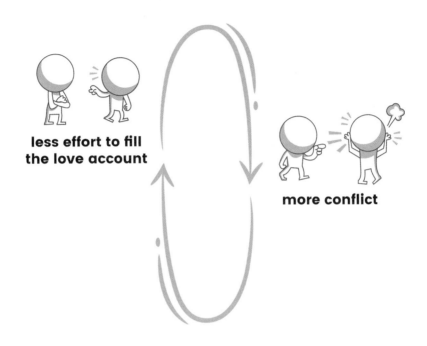

**less effort to fill
the love account**

more conflict

unfortunately far too common for many couples. If you're starting to see that you might have been deprioritizing your partnership,
you're not alone, but it is time to make a change.

The truth is, it can be easy to unconsciously take your partnership for granted and put in less effort. Sure, you might say "thank
you" when they cook you dinner, or do something in the backyard,
but that doesn't necessarily mean you're putting in your A-game,
and filling the love account. Think back to the beginning of your
relationship for a minute. You were extremely excited to see them,
so you made sure you looked nice, you listened to them attentively
at dinner, you kissed them on the cheek, grabbed their hand, and
complimented them for the things you adored. Your effort was high
because there was the anticipation of things going well and it turning into a long-term and loving relationship. You could say that you

wanted to be "successful" in them liking you and sticking with you. So, you took more actions that filled the love account. But you don't fill up your car once with gas (or nowadays plug in your electric car to charge just once), you must do this frequently. This is the same in your relationship and your love account.

But as time went on, and things didn't feel quite *as* exciting as they did in the beginning, your effort went down. Look, it's not because you have bad intentions or anything! That's a funny thing that human beings do in all areas of life. You're initially excited about something new, you then acquire it or experience it, but then it just becomes familiar and a normal part of life. When something becomes "normal," the effort and enthusiasm starts to go down. For example, think about how excited you are when you get a new car! You wash and clean it every day, you park miles away from any cars in the parking lot, and you want to show it to everyone! Then about six months to a year after that you throw trash in the back of it, let dust settle on the dashboard, and only detail the interior every few months.

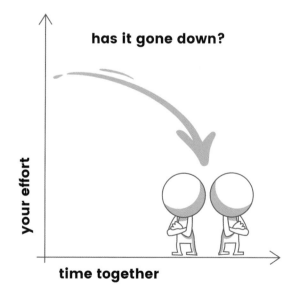

What many couples tend to do to compensate for the daily declining excitement and/or effort is take periodic big vacations or buy gifts. Now, don't get us wrong, we love a good vacation! But going on a trip once or twice per year, or scheduling one date night each month, will not make up for a lack of daily effort. Can you get and stay fit only going to the gym four times per year or eating one salad per month? Obviously not, so why would you rely on infrequent actions for your relationship to keep your love account full? A common misconception we hear from couples is "that's why we keep up our monthly date nights." But that's not going to be what fills your love account either because it's not about the "size" of the action but the frequency!

The Gottman Institute calls small gestures and attempts to connect with your partner a "bid." Some examples of bids are: a kiss on the cheek, a tap on the butt, a compliment, starting a conversation, etc. A legend in the relationship research world, John Gottman, found that the longevity of a relationship relies heavily on how often a couple makes and turns toward each other's bids.[2] He didn't find that it was related to the number of gifts given, vacations taken, or any elaborate actions. It was actually the accumulation of all of the tiny attempts to connect with each other that filled their love account. The Gottman Institute's research proves that what you and your partner actually care about deep down, and what actually makes you feel loved and connected, are the consistent small things. They are often so small that you wouldn't even think it contributes that much to your relationship . . . but it does! These tiny efforts often decline over time and you unconsciously take your relationship for granted. You may have even said something like "don't you just know I love you?"

---

2 Gottman, John M. *The Relationship Cure*. New York: Three Rivers Press, 2001.

At this point, some couples allow their low love accounts to linger and avoid acknowledging the disconnected feeling by keeping "busy" and distracting themselves with other areas of life. You know, with housework, taking care of kids, advancing in their professions, and all the barbecue and birthday party invitations. If that experience continues for months or years, you can start to feel numb and resigned; even worse, it can lead to ending the relationship because of how low your love accounts get.

It can feel especially challenging to fill your love account when it's really low because you don't "feel" like putting in the effort. Especially if you feel like your partner isn't putting in the effort either. Now both of you are in a stalemate waiting to see who will take the initiative to reconnect first, which can go on and on. (Since you are reading this book, guess who should take the lead by going first?)

You're likely wondering *how do we fill the love account and keep it full?* You do that through making frequent deposits (bids, as John Gottman says) into your partner's love account. Just like your

DEPOSITS:

- compliments
- a kiss on the cheek
- appreciation
- a tap on the butt
- attempting sexual intimacy
- an act of service
- paying attention to them

WITHDRAWALS:

- criticism
- withholding physical affection
- ignoring what they said
- rejecting physical affection
- passive aggressive language
- short replies or lack of conversation
- being distracted while they talk

financial bank account thrives when you make more frequent financial deposits, so does your relationship love account. On the contrary, if you make more withdrawals than deposits, your account will go down (and can even hit zero). Above are some examples of simple deposits or withdrawals to your love account.

It isn't realistic for your love accounts to always be 100 percent full, or that you'll never make withdrawals from it. Instead, the goal is to bring awareness to the fact that you both have a love account, and to be intentional about making more frequent deposits than you do withdrawals. Instead of having to guess or assume how your partner feels, ask each other weekly "how full is your love account right now?" or "what type of deposits (actions) do you prefer to fill your love account?" Make it a part of your vocabulary and check in on each other's account levels at least once per week. Don't wait for your partner to ask you . . . be proactive and speak up if your own love account is low!

Here's the thing, you might be making withdrawals from your love account that you aren't aware of. Let's say you catch yourself making a condescending remark about the way they completed something around the house. Well, you can counteract the negative effect of those remarks by doubling down on making a few deposits afterward. It's important to recognize, however, that you can't use deposits as a crutch for being unaware of how often you make withdrawals. You must also take responsibility for getting to the root cause of why you might be doing that.

For this before-conflict strategy, the goal is to make frequent "deposits" to each other's love accounts because it helps build your connection and prevents having an Argument Hangover. Conflicts seem more significant when your account is low. If you had a bank account with $500,000 and you made a $1,000 withdrawal, it wouldn't feel like a big deal. However, if you had $1,500 in your account and the same $1,000 withdrawal happened, you may be really worried, reactionary, or panicked. These are the same type of feelings you have when it comes to conflicts in your relationship when your love account is low. If you encounter seasons where you are arguing a lot or you feel disconnected, remember to focus on the small daily deposits that will strengthen your connection and love.

DRIVE-BY CONVERSATIONS AND GETTING BLINDSIDED

Every time we host one of our in-person couples workshops, we ask each couple that we meet these two questions:

1. What was your main reason for attending? (To which they 95 percent of the time respond with "to work on communication and conflict resolution.")
2. When was the last time you put active attention toward your relationship? (To which 80 percent of couples say "never, we've been too busy." The other 20 percent of couples say they either tried counseling and it wasn't giving them the results they wanted, or that they haven't done any relationship "work" since preparing for marriage.)

Even though we've heard it thousands of times, we still find it fascinating, or more so concerning, that couples feel they've been too busy to work on the relationship. You don't need to be a rocket scientist to see that modern-day life has added immense complexity and pressure to your life and relationship. You not only are trying to figure out how to take care of yourself, but you each have dozens of other roles you're expected to play in life.

As you can see from the graphic below, you each have a long list of roles you're expected to play. You're already tired when you get done with your work day, whether that's your profession or taking care of the family, and you still have many other responsibilities that require your attention. Couples say to us all the time, "I feel like we don't have anything left for each other at the end of the day." Here are just a few roles you may find yourself playing:

Riley, in any given day is playing the role of:

- Mom
- Wife
- Sister
- Lover
- Career Title
- Dish Cleaner
- Laundry-Doer
- Fitness Instructor
- Cook/ Nutritionist
- Friend
- Family Activities Director
- House Cleaner
- Business Owner

Parker, in any given day is playing the role of:

- Dad
- Husband
- Brother
- Intimacy Initiator
- CFO of the Bills
- Grocery Shopper
- Job Position/ Title
- Mediator
- Investor
- Problem Solver (coach)
- Handyman
- Therapist
- Chauffeur for kids

And this table doesn't even count many of the other modern life distractions: your cell phone, social media platforms, the amount of overwhelming news and media, the pressure to show up to all social and family gatherings, and more. In fact, what do so many people say when you ask how they are? "Oh, we're good, just super *busy*." It's like a badge of honor to be that busy. Somewhere success got redefined to be the sheer amount of action and activity you could take, even if that means sacrificing the quality and satisfaction in your relationship. This can even be said for relational connection as a whole in society. For many, it's become more important to fill the schedule with activity than to form authentic relationships, so at the end of the day you find yourselves trying to connect, but the conversation just turns into a rundown of the tasks completed that day. "How did your meeting go? What do you want for dinner? How were the kids today? What show is on tonight?" But those questions don't end up feeling like they connect the two of you; and if you're really honest, they become very routine.

Modern life pressures dominate a good portion of your energy, leaving just the scraps left over for your partner. How does this relate to before-conflict strategies? Well, these pressures contribute to conflicts in two main ways:

1. You can feel so much pressure and overload that you are shorter-tempered and reactive to your partner.
2. You don't have the time (or make the time) for meaningful conversations, so you end up having what we call "drive-by conversations."

Drive-by conversations are those moments when you're trying to squeeze in a conversation while multitasking. It's an unplanned, spur-of-the-moment conversation you want to have that can feel like an interruption to your partner. This could be while getting dressed in the morning, making breakfast for your kids, or packing your bag to head to work. Drive-by conversations can also be those moments when you try to squeeze in a conversation right before going to bed. You're both exhausted, but you roll over toward your partner and say "so, we need to talk about . . ."

There are so many distinct conversations with couples that we've coached where their main source of communication existed solely on drive-by conversations. No wonder they felt conversations never really got complete and that conflicts would linger for days. One couple in particular, Hayden and Alexis, was trying to understand why seemingly simple conversations would turn into a three-hour heated fight, poor sleep, and then remorse and pain in the mornings. While their conflict dynamic of course involved several factors, one major culprit was that they were always having drive-by conversations at the end of the day. By the time they came home from work, cooked dinner, bathed the kids, cleaned up the house, and watched a thirty-minute show to relax, they were utterly exhausted! They would lay down in bed and one person would have a couple of things they needed to talk about. Within minutes, they would both get defensive and resentful that they were having an important conversation right before trying to sleep. Neither of them was feeling understood, and in fact, they were both feeling rejected and isolated. If it was an especially sensitive topic for them, it would then escalate and drag into the next day. We explained to them that this falls into the category of a drive-by conversation.

While it might seem like that's the only time you two have to talk, it's not the best time to talk about important or sensitive matters. You see, a drive-by conversation increases your odds of getting defensive, short-tempered, or reactionary as one or both of you feels bombarded. We call that bombarded experience being "blindsided." Just like when you're driving and you can't see a car coming, which feels like it came out of nowhere, you can feel blindsided by your partner bringing up a topic out of nowhere. When you're in a driver's ed class, you're taught to be aware of peoples' blind spots and to use your blinker to alert and cue other drivers around you of where you're moving. This is obviously with the goal of safe driving and not getting into a collision.

We'll assume you're a great driver and always abide by these driving rules, but how are you when it comes to alerting your partner before you bring up a potentially triggering topic? While you might not be able to completely remove modern-day pressures from your life, you do have the ability to eliminate drive-by conversations. First off, you must schedule the time to have important conversations. Don't let being busy and not having enough time be an excuse for blindsiding your partner.

If you want to have a particular conversation about your finances, intimacy, or topics around your kids, ask your partner if now is a good time to have that conversation. Don't just start talking because you just now thought of it and *you* want to talk about it now. For now, just start to bring attention to the moments you're about to initiate a drive-by conversation.

If you need to talk about something, say to your partner "hey, is now a good time to talk about _____?" You could also say "is now a good time for me to talk with you about _____ (the subject)?" Depending on the timing or how in-depth the conversation would need to go, your partner might say anything from "yes, now is a good time to talk," "I am free to talk in 10 minutes," or even "can we set up a time to talk about this tomorrow after work?" This is what we call a "permission based" conversation. Now, don't misread that, we don't mean permission in the sense that your partner runs the show. Getting their "permission" means getting their buy-in and "yes" to being ready to talk about something. This is extremely powerful when it comes to not blindsiding your partner.

> Remember that one of the subtle causes of conflict is that you blindside your partner because you're trying to squeeze in a conversation.

Beware of the times you two are so busy that you try to talk about something important while getting ready for the day, making your kids' lunches, or packing your bag for work. These drive-by conversations are what can blindside you both, and lead to unnecessary conflicts and Argument Hangovers.

THE "WEEKLY FAMILY MEETING" CHECK-IN

In this section, we'll go in-depth about a very practical tool you can implement for scheduling time to talk about matters you didn't have time to during the week, but more specifically to check in on your relationship. We call this time together a "weekly family meeting." Imagine being able to prevent conflicts from starting because you catch things before they snowball into a bigger issue. Unfortunately, we live in a reactive society in many ways: only going to the doctor once you are really sick, only seeking counsel/going to therapy once you're in total crisis, or going to the gym once you are huffing and puffing for air walking up the stairs.

In your relationship, conflicts are often manifestations of things getting missed because you didn't have a "tune up" or "check-in time." By the time some issues are brought up, there can be so much resentment and pain infused into the conflict that it leads to a blow-out fight or even divorce. This resentment comes from prolonged low love accounts, drive-by conversations, lack of family check-ins, and painful Argument Hangovers.

A recent movie portrayed this unfortunate truth brilliantly. Spoiler alert if you haven't seen the movie *The Marriage Story* with Scarlett Johansson and Adam Driver yet.

This was the *best* worst movie we have seen! Let's be a little clearer for you: this movie was incredibly well made and acted. It was impressive how they both are able to feel and elicit emotion, many times right in a moment. But it was the worst movie for the lack of simple relationship tools and skills, poor communication, and withholding important things from each other until it was "too late." It also portrays the way the majority of couples handle conflict and keep themselves all too frequently in the Argument Hangover.

What stood out to us while watching the movie was how long the wife, Nicole Barber (Scarlett's character), withheld her true feelings and suffering from her husband, Charlie Barber (Adam's character). She was silently resenting him for the lack of contribution to his playwriting company, and feeling emotionally distant for *years* before she finally revealed it to him. Unfortunately, he was massively blindsided when she wanted to move forward with a divorce. Her character believed that Charlie should have known she was unhappy all along. (Which also portrays how often people expect their partner to read their minds, even though we all know the cliché saying, "they can't read your mind.") Of course, this wasn't just Nicole's fault that she didn't bring up her discontent. Charlie didn't do everything he could to make sure they were on the same page. He didn't pause throughout their years together and ask her how she felt about her level of contribution, love account level, or relationship satisfaction. He made assumptions that she was happy. And how can you ever really know anything if you do not ask, right?

They ultimately went forward with the divorce because she wanted it. Her desire for the divorce, as for many others, was created because of the silent, withheld communication that built up into a pile of resentment. That resentment became so potent that it felt like it could not be repaired. (Her love account was below empty!)

While this movie shows how many couples end up splitting, it also portrayed the unwillingness to learn, practice, and implement the necessary and simple skills that could have kept the divorce from happening. Yet it's not even really about the divorce but the pain they cause each other, their families, and their son in the process. Even for the characters, they just didn't know what skills they needed and their challenges felt very personal to them. Many couples think that their challenges mean something is wrong with *them* (and that it's unfixable), instead of realizing that they're just missing key tools and skills.

Put yourself in their shoes for a minute. When was the last time you checked in on your relationship? Not just a to-do list of what needs to be done each week for your house to operate, but an emotional check-in for all areas of your relationship to see how satisfied you each are. For most couples we've coached, they either have never done a relationship check-in, or they would ask a general question like "you're happy in the relationship, right?" If you're in the latter boat of asking a general question, kudos to you for attempting some sort of a constructive conversation. But now is the time to take that even further. This principle will take your positive intent to the next level, because even if you have asked your partner "are you happy in the relationship," they might be satisfied in some but not all areas of your relationship. Wherever you fall, it's critical to implement a more specific, organized check-in because there are distinct and equally important areas within your relationship. The two most common offenses we see in this context are:

- Assuming your partner is generally happy and satisfied.
- Not sharing your feelings and expecting your partner to somehow know when you're not satisfied in a particular core area of the relationship.

Expecting your partner to read your mind is only a great strategy if you're married to a psychic; and even then, it's just not very partnership-like. If you're like us (not married to a psychic), continue on. Worry not, there's a solution for you, and it's called the weekly family meeting, your safe zone to:

- Audit each area of your relationship (we'll list nine areas below).
- Share your satisfaction level without judging or getting defensive to each other's answers.
- Gain an understanding of how your partner is feeling and what they need.
- Identify a goal or intention for that area to boost your satisfaction as a couple.
- Catch any disappointments before they build up into something bigger, triggering conflict and resentment.

So, what do you do in this weekly family meeting? Let's take it step-by-step:

1. Block at least 30 to 60 minutes to sit down for this conversation (once you get the hang of the process, you could do your weekly family meeting on a walk).
2. Do everything you can to remove all distractions (phones, computers, TV, kids).
3. Agree that you are in a "safe zone" before you start. You both must commit to share authentically and listen to each other to understand, not react.
4. Grab a piece of paper and a pen (or download the weekly family meeting worksheet from our website MeetTheFreemans.com).
5. There should be three columns on your piece of paper (or the downloaded PDF). In the left-hand column, write "Area of relationship." For the middle column, write "Each of our satisfaction scores 1–10." And for the right-hand column, write "Our goal/intention for this area."

Area of Relationship	Each of our satisfaction scores 1–10	Our goal/intention for this area

6. Now, for the left-hand column under "Area of relationship," there will be nine rows for the nine areas of your relationship: Communication, Family, Financial, Intimacy, Mindset/Emotional, Physical, Professional, Social, and Spiritual.
7. Once you're set up to begin the meeting:
   A. Go down through each of the nine areas of the relationship, sharing your satisfaction level (1–10). Each of you will give a score in all nine areas.
   B. You both will need to listen non-defensively, to understand first and not to react or make it about you. Then

you can share a little more detail about the areas for which you have lower scores so your partner can better understand. Some helpful prompts for each other: Tell me a little more about why you scored our intimacy a 5 out of 10; I'd love to understand what made your spiritual score go down from last week; please share with me what was missing in the area of communication for it to be a 6 for you.

C. Once you both feel that you've shared some more context for your score, together create a goal/intention for each area. You'll want to create a goal/intention even if you had a higher score like a 9 or 10 for that area so that you keep it high. Perhaps spend more time creating the goal for the two or three that had the lowest satisfaction scores. We'll elaborate more on what the goals/intentions could look like in just a minute.

D. Keep your worksheet in a visible place so that you are reminded of your goals/intentions over the next week.

E. Hug, embrace, and celebrate that you had a meaningful check-in for your relationship! Remember that no matter what was shared, it was going that way already. So now you know, and this has brought you together on the same page!

Since you might be more used to creating personal goals for your health or career, let's dive more into what a goal/intention would look like in the areas of your relationship. First things first, it might take some banter back and forth to create a goal/intention that is aligned for both of you. Don't give up if at first your partner doesn't resonate with one that you throw out there as a suggestion. Write down a few ideas and then, together, select one that feels the most like a win-win for the week. Remember that it's not the one week that makes all the difference, it's the compounded effect of week after week after week. So if one week the goal is something that's a bit more important to your partner, remember that next week the goal could lean more toward your preferences. You're a team, remember?

The reason column 3 says "goal/intention" and not just goal is because sometimes an intention is needed more than a specific goal. You likely have heard that a goal is only useful if it's specific. For instance, if you're going to create a goal for intimacy, it must be more specific than you think for it to be clear to both of you. For example, setting the goal to be physically intimate two more times each week. An intention might resonate more sometimes because it allows for more wiggle room on how you both will express it. The late Dr. Wayne Dyer said "our intention creates our reality." You might use the phrase "they don't have good intentions," but do you really pause and set intentions yourself? Are you clear on what your intentions are in the relationship? In our experience with setting intentions almost every single week (and sometimes even daily) for seven years, they plant a seed in our minds that, if we nurture, starts to drive our actions. For example, you could set the intention to be "more playful and creative" in the area of "Family." Then, you could think of things to do like planning a picnic for the weekend, playing board games together instead of watching TV, or taking short breaks in the day to run around the yard with the dog. While intentions might seem vague to some, if you keep that in your awareness through saying it out loud a few times each day, putting a visual reminder on your phone, or putting the worksheet on your refrigerator to see each morning, it will start to influence your thinking. Your intentions are only as powerful as your level of commitment and how present you keep them in your awareness. Your decision to be intentional is one of the most powerful forces on earth for producing new results in life!

In the context of your weekly family meeting, your intention could be more about how you will *be* toward each other. In other words, your way of being. Think of those times that you say to your partner "gosh, you're being so sensitive" or "you're being so harsh with me." You're referring to their way of being rather than their particular actions. In all moments, all times, you are exuding "a way of being." Consciously or unconsciously, you're *being* kind, mean, playful, apathetic, loving, harsh, creative, or any of the other hundreds of ways of "being."

So, if you're going to set an intention instead of a goal for an area of your relationship, make it about how you will both *be* with each other. Here are a few clear examples:

1. In the area of communication, we intend to *be open, patient, and clear* in everything we say to each other this week.
2. In the area of intimacy, we intend to *be assertive, creative, and enthusiastic* with each other in the intimate space this week.
3. In the area of finances, we intend to *be resourceful, organized, and structured* with how we spend and make money this week.

These example intentions could be starkly different than how you two are being with each other now. When we did this exercise with one couple married for ten years, Reese and Emerson, they had never set intentions (or even goals) for their relationship. They were just assuming that things would work themselves out and love would just always "be there." The two big areas they chose to work on were communication and intimacy. We asked Reese, "How would you describe your overall attitude or way of being in the area of intimacy?" To which he replied, "boring and apathetic for sure." We then asked Emerson how she was being in the area of communication and she said "definitely condescending and passive aggressive." We acknowledged them for being so authentic and willing to own it. For their weekly family meeting, we encouraged them to set intentions for a couple of weeks before setting clear goals. Together, they created an intention for those two areas.

For intimacy: "We intend to be curious and assertive in our intimacy this week."

For communication: "We intend to be proactive and calm in our communication this week."

They went home and placed those intentions in their bathroom to see at least a couple of times per day, and they also said they were committed to those intentions. Remember, an intention doesn't just make something happen magically, you have to be committed to it. Two weeks later, we had another virtual session with them and they seemed visibly different. They were physically closer together, smiling at each other more, and they both seemed happier as individuals. They shared that of course things weren't perfect (perfect would be boring), but that their intimacy and communication were the best they had been in over five years. They both found ways to be more assertive and curious in their intimacy, even if in small ways. But they said it was the small things that added up to it feeling totally different for them. For communication, they still had moments where they reacted too quickly, but they reminded themselves to be more proactive and they talked about things way sooner than they normally would. Reese and Emerson said they would continue to set intentions for a couple more weeks, then move to creating more specific goals. They finally felt progress in the relationship! Imagine what intentions can do for your relationship. Just take a moment to notice if you haven't been aware of your way of being, and how that might be impacting your partner. No blame or self-pity, but just self-awareness.

Before you start your weekly family meeting as a couple, here are examples of specific goal setting, instead of intention setting, that could be set for each area of the relationship. To say "let's work on communication" is not a goal! That's not even an intention, that's just saying you hope things will get better. If you're going to set a goal for communication, or any other area of your relationship, it has to be written in a way that you both know how you're "winning." In fact, a common point of tension we witness with couples stems from how they see "progress" differently. One partner might think that great intimacy is about how frequently sex occurs, while the other person might not care about frequency at all, but more so about how thoughtful the moment felt (like with candles, music, etc.). Even think about those moments you say to your partner "I'd like it if we worked on our finances." And the other person says, "Yeah, let's do that." But you two might see "working on your finances" as meaning two completely different things.

That's why you'll want to create these goals in the SMART format. You may remember this from the good old days at school: a SMART goal is specific, measurable, attainable, relevant, and time-based. And yes, it is completely possible to create SMART goals for the different areas of your relationship, even if it feels odd for a moment. Here are some examples for each area of the relationship:

- **Communication:** We commit to sit down once per week for 3 months for the weekly family meeting and we will each take turns talking and listening for 3 to 5 minutes.
- **Family:** We will all have dinner at the table without any phones 3 nights per week.
- **Financial:** We will add up all of our monthly expenses (all bills and credit cards) and find $300 to remove.
- **Intimacy:** We will each initiate sexual intimacy one time per week, and one time per week will involve candles and music.
- **Mindset/Emotional:** We will each select a personal development book to read at night for 15 minutes before we sleep (like the one you are reading now)!
- **Professional:** We will block our calendars after 5 p.m. so that late meetings don't pop up last minute that keep us working all the time.

- **Physical:** We will exercise together for 30 minutes per day, 5 days per week. And only eat out twice per week.
- **Social:** We will set up double date nights one time per month, doing some kind of unique activity and not just eating at a restaurant.
- **Spiritual:** We will attend a group or type of church of our choice twice per month, and learn to meditate 5 minutes each day.

Those are just examples and your list will likely look different, but the point is that it feels like a win-win goal to both of you, which does not include settling or a show of force for either party. It also must feel genuinely attainable to you and not making such a leap that you give up after a day. Think about increasing the "goal" by just 5 percent week to week, which compounds into massive changes over time. If you set your expectations too high in every area of the relationship, it can feel overwhelming and unrealistic.

For each of the listed areas, should you set an intention or a goal? There's no right or wrong if you choose to set an intention versus a goal. Try a few of each and see which feels more impactful week to week. The part that's critical is that you continue to have these family meetings over time because your needs likely change, especially in different seasons and circumstances. You don't just want to have a few family meetings and think you "know" what your partner needs because it might be different in a month or a year. What you want or need could even be different next week. You are ever changing and evolving people, and so will be your needs and desires. Now, get ready to start your family meeting check-ins!

YOUR GAME PLAN

- Sit down and create your agreements/ground rules for times of conflict. Put them in a visible place for reminders until they become natural for you.
- Focus on making frequent deposits to your partner's love account and bring awareness to the ways you've unconsciously made withdrawals.
- Identify the times that you initiate drive-by conversations that are interruptions to your partner and create defensiveness.
- Schedule your weekly family meetings within the next 14 days and another for the end of the month to start to make it a regular habit.

> You can fight smarter and shorten the Argument Hangover by proactively creating agreements, filling your love account, and having intentional conversations.

6

DURING CONFLICT

"First seek to understand before being understood."
—Stephen Covey

The whistle has blown and now it's "game time" aka you're in the heat of a disagreement. Now, if you implement what you read in the last few chapters, you will have less frequent and less emotionally heightened conflicts. But you're human and always will be, so this chapter will then be especially helpful for the times disagreements do come up!

Jocelyn wasn't much of an athlete growing up, but I (Aaron) was passionate and skilled at multiple sports through my college years. As with any athlete, I didn't become good at basketball overnight; it took practice day in and day out (by my calculations about 20,000 hours in total now). My coaches would give me feedback about the position of my feet or elbow when shooting a free throw, the defensive stance and shuffling of my feet when guarding someone one-on-one, and how to know when to make the right pass versus taking the shot. I wanted to be a better teammate, so I committed to learning and practicing the right individual skills over and over, to better serve the team.

Sports analogy or not, one of the most important aspects for a successful team is not to let your ego block you from owning up to where you aren't skilled enough. This is just as true when it comes to "fighting" in your relationship, and we invite you to embrace learning these relationship skills during conflict, just like you would if you cared about becoming a better teammate at work, basketball, or even as an online gamer!

The truth is, you're probably not very "good" at fighting and need to hone your skills to be a better partner during conflict. But you're not alone. In fact, Jesse from our community said "I seem to get defensive really quickly and after that I shut down and don't look at anything from her perspective. Then nothing is solved and it's weird for a couple days." This chapter is all about how you can be more skilled during the "fight" so that it actually leads to becoming closer, instead of pushing you apart. As we shared earlier in the book, conflict can actually make you stronger together. Conflict can be constructive and help you learn new things about each other, create new solutions and possibilities for your life, and lead to you both growing as individuals. But only if you learn how to fight smarter. This is the chapter to help you do just that.

Early on in our marriage we would reach moments in the argument when we literally paused and said "wait, what are we fighting about again?" You've likely had those moments when you forgot the original topic because you started to fight about *how* you were fighting. It looks like this five minutes into the argument:

"Don't yell at me! You're being a jerk!"

"You know what, I am about to leave if you keep talking to me like a child!"

"I didn't call you a child, you just act like one."

"Stop raising your voice! The kids can hear!"

"Wait, what were we talking about in the first place?"

Notice how the back and forth started to become about managing each other during the conflict. Sometimes the original cause of the conflict was really only of 3/10 importance to you, but how you both acted during the conflict made it hurtful and took it to an 8/10. Now you're not disagreeing about the cause, but you're hurt by the tactics used, or lack thereof. What you need are better skills so that you don't cause more harm during the conflict, and you can actually get back to resolving the difference of opinion it all started from. First, we'll start with two seemingly simple but often missed skills, then dive into four that require more practice and a commitment to master them.

SELF-AWARENESS OF YOUR BODY AND BODY LANGUAGE

Most people get so lost in their emotions and become completely unaware of how they're acting during a conflict—the emotional trigger cycle. You can become so fixated on your partner and what they're saying and doing that you have no idea how you're acting in those moments. The skills we teach below will be useless to you if you aren't self-aware. As you read that you might think *well, that sounds nice, but how do I become more self-aware during an argument?* It is a wonderful question because you have to realize that you, as a human being, are not designed to be a great "fighter" or self-aware when emotions run high.

Daniel Goleman coined a powerful term to describe this problem and called it the "amygdala hijack" in his book *Emotional Intelligence*. We briefly referred to this on page 64 to talk about emotional triggers and triggered behavior. This term refers to a personal, emotional response that is immediate, overwhelming, and out of measure with the actual stimulus because it has triggered a much more significant emotional threat. When you aren't aware of this term, you can easily lose awareness of how you're talking, standing, moving, or even your facial expressions. It's called "hijacking" because it feels like something else took over your body, and you aren't choosing what you're saying and doing. It's almost as if your body has a mind of its own.

However, if you're committed to becoming more self-aware, you can manage this hijacking and choose a different set of actions in those moments. It's not easy, but you can. In our work with couples, we emphasize the importance of implementing the following steps, even before you try to add new communication skills into the mix:

1. **Breathe:** It might seem so simple, but people start breathing really shallow when they're in an emotional state. If you focus on breathing in for three seconds and out for three seconds, it will help bring your awareness back to the present moment and into your body again. Even try it right now and you'll see how quickly you can shift your focus.

2. **Slow down:** If you become "hijacked" but you focus on slowing down your responses, it will lend to more constructive outcomes. Even if your partner says something that bothers you, count to three before you say something back. You don't need to react right away. Give yourself a few seconds to respond.

3. **Ask yourself these questions:** What am I feeling? Where am I feeling this emotion in my body? Am I acting how I really want to toward my partner? Am I breathing enough? How do I want this argument to really go? What is the real goal here with my partner?

4. **Body language:** Stand or sit in a more open, less defensive position. Without knowing it, your body language and your emotions are linked together and can influence each other. If you're mad, you tend to cross your arms and slump. If you're happy, you tend to have your shoulders back and arms open. You can influence your feelings by changing your body language, so even if you're mad, put your arms down and keep your body turned toward your partner. If you really want to be more advanced, even try smiling for a second and you can actually release "happy chemicals" in your body (endorphins, oxytocin, serotonin, dopamine). It's also important to be aware if your body language starts to appear aggressive, which can signify the release of the stress/survival chemicals (adrenaline and cortisol). For example, waving your arms, making

aggressive movements, pointing fingers, or turning your back on them only escalates your emotions and causes the same rush of chemicals in their body. This creates an environment that feels shut down, closed off, and unsafe for you both. As you practice being more self-aware, keep your body language in a more peaceful and relaxed state: shoulders down and back, arms uncrossed, movements slow, and face muscles relaxed.

The goal of understanding the "amygdala hijack" and practicing more self-awareness is that you are able to observe yourself and shift your behavior no matter what emotions you're feeling. You won't be perfect at this from the start, but you will see compounded benefits of practicing this over the next months and years. Over time, you'll be able to feel any emotion (anger, sadness, guilt, etc.) while also being aware of how you're letting it influence your body's reactions. It's like being a fly on the wall and watching yourself from above. You can become a master of yourself and choose the actions that will best serve your relationship.

DOES SOMEONE NEED TO CALL A TIME-OUT?

The next step after becoming more self-aware during an argument is to recognize when you two need to take a pause or "time-out." Do you remember on page 81 when we talked about setting an agreement not to storm out of the room without saying when you'll be back? Requesting to take a time-out can be another part of implementing this agreement.

If you have a tendency to storm out of the room or shut down, the time-out is going to be especially helpful for you. But it doesn't work to just leave or pick up your phone to distract yourself. When you abruptly leave the room, it's more likely an escape to avoid feeling the not-so-pleasant emotions. This can potentially leave your partner feeling abandoned and shut out. Imagine if you just got up and left a meeting with your boss and colleagues . . . that would be rude and possibly disrespectful—you might even get fired! Any team member, whether that's at work or at home, wants to know that you won't just abruptly "quit" by walking out without at least saying that you will be coming back! Ultimately, there's nothing wrong with needing a break to calm down, gather yourself, or process the emotion that is coming up for you. In fact, many people do process their emotions privately (which we'll talk more about later on). The key difference is about communicating your needs to your partner.

- Walking out = a reactive and fear-based attempt to escape and avoid the moment, which leaves your partner feeling isolated and in the dark.
- Requesting a time-out = a powerfully requested and agreed upon pause with the commitment to being able to come back to love and connection.

The biggest difference here is that you're communicating your need for a pause in a respectful manner, rather than just quitting on the conversation by walking out (especially with a snarky comment to get the last word in). The importance of this cannot be understated: if your partner calls a time-out, you have to honor it right in that moment. Don't keep talking to try to get your last word in. It is detrimental to keep throwing out painful statements once your partner requests a time-out because it's crossing a healthy boundary. Continuing to talk at your partner or denying their request to take the time-out only perpetuates the fight and is unfair. It's like hitting a boxing opponent right in the gut after the bell rang. Not only is it a clear disregard for the rules but has the potential to be very harmful. Here's a guide to request a time-out and honor it in a healthy way:

1. You *notice* your emotions are escalating, things are not going anywhere constructive, and you need a pause to calm down emotionally.

111

2. You *calmly say* something like, "Let's just pause, I need to request a time-out." (If you at least get to this step and both honor the agreement for the time-out, this is a total win!)

3. Indicate *how long* of a break you are requesting and what you are going to do. "I am requesting a time-out for thirty minutes and I'll be in the other room (or I'm going to go for a walk around the block and will be back)."

4. An advanced step is to tell your partner what your *commitment* is for taking the time-out. "I am committed to coming back together to understand each other and get on the same page again."

5. This part is now critical: you must either come back together at the time you promised to complete the conversation, or at least communicate if you need to request an extension of time.

It's imperative that you understand the importance of coming back together at the time you both promised. Why? Because if you don't, you both lose trust in each other and it degrades this foundational element of your partnership. If you need additional time because you genuinely still need a moment to reflect, process, or calm down, let them know so they're not left in the dark wondering. The power of requesting a time-out is that it helps prevent you from saying or doing things that cause an Argument Hangover.

COMMUNICATION SKILLS

Now that you're focusing on becoming more self-aware during a conflict, and identifying when a time-out is required, let's move into how to be better communicators. If we cut to the chase, the cold-hard truth would be that your communication skills really need an upgrade. This advice is not only for you, because we *all* should seek to be better communicators. Communication is such a dynamic topic that frankly requires a completely separate book of its own, but we'll cover some of the most critical communication techniques needed during a conflict here.

The only way that this section will make a difference for you is if you remember that you must recognize and own your personal triggers so that you can focus on actually communicating and not just reacting. You see, communicating in a conflict can't be filled with you spewing all of your thoughts and emotions at your partner or you fighting tooth and nail for your viewpoint to be right. When we sit with couples and witness an argument get triggered, we notice the exact moment when they are no longer communicating and when they start just talking *at* each other.

There is a very big difference between those two things: actually communicating versus talking at each other. Talking at each other involves cutting your partner off before they finish a sentence, making assumptions about the meaning of what they are saying, no longer listening to what is actually being said, and trying to one-up your partner so that you come out as the "winner." Talking at each other can sound like this:

Partner 1: "Can you please do a better job cleaning up your crap? How many times do I have to ask you?"

Partner 2: "Seriously, you're going to attack me for these socks on the ground right after I come home from work? Do you know how hard I work?"

Partner 1: "Oh, so you don't think I work as hard as you do? You think your days are harder and longer than mine are? See, you don't appreciate my efforts at all!"

In this scenario, the two of them might think they're communicating, but they aren't. They are talking *at* each other. Partner 1 was not clear or kind in their request, and partner 2 interpreted one statement as something that wasn't really being said. This brings us to the first communication skill you can focus on during times of conflict to shorten or avoid the Argument Hangover altogether.

FOCUS ON ACTUALLY LISTENING

You could potentially overlook the immense benefit here when you read the line about "actually listening," because it isn't news to you that you could work on being a better listener. But the problem is that most people know that they could be a better listener, but don't know how. Why is this? Because you're not trained to listen with the intention to understand, which is the true purpose of communication, especially when you get flooded with emotion and your survival instincts kick in. To make it easier for you to master listening and understanding each other, we'll break it down into three categories for you to become aware of: not listening at all, just hearing, and actual listening.

	Not listening at all	Just hearing	Actual listening
The difference	Getting emotionally triggered, automatically reacting, making assumptions about what they "mean," forcing your point of view.	Your ears hear what your partner says, but you're unwilling to empathize, see their point of view, or understand where they are coming from.	When you focus on understanding them first, not necessarily agreeing, but you empathize with what they are feeling and validate their perspective.
Example 1	Partner 1 says: "Can't you do a better job cleaning up after yourself?" Partner 2 reacts: "Seriously, you're going to give me a hard time after I worked hard today?"	Partner 1 says: "Can't you do a better job cleaning up after yourself?" Partner 2 says: "Yes, I heard you the first time, get off my back about it!"	Partner 1 says: "Can't you do a better job cleaning up after yourself?" Partner 2: "It sounds like you are upset, so this must be important to you. Tell me more about what you mean by cleaning up in particular."

	Not listening at all	Just hearing	Actual listening
Example 2	Partner 1 says: "Can't you turn off the TV so we can actually spend time together?" Partner 2 reacts: "Why are you nagging me about this, do you not get enough attention or something?"	Partner 1 says: "Can't you turn off the TV so we can actually spend time together?" Partner 2 says: "This is like the fourth time you have said this, I told you I would in thirty minutes."	Partner 1 says: "Can't you turn off the TV so we can actually spend time together?" Partner 2: "I would like to spend time with you too. I've been looking forward to this show all week, so how about we do X together right after?"

In these examples it's obvious that Partner 1 wasn't communicating well and could have made their request in a kinder manner. Plus, this was more of a drive-by conversation and they could have also asked if it was a good time for their partner to talk. Yet this section is about listening. Sometimes your partner will get caught up in something and say things in a way that feels rude, but you still have the ability to respond differently as the listener.

As you can see in the table, there is a big difference between not listening at all, just audibly hearing the words of your partner, and actually listening. Unfortunately, when people say they're "working on communication," they're only focused on talking more but only get to the level of just hearing the words. While it's a step up from being reactive, it still lacks the level of attention and empathy to have your partner feel understood. Without empathy, you will not be able to turn your conflicts into a benefit. We'll even hear some partners say "I hear you; you don't have to say it twice." The reason your partner repeats themselves is because the elements of understanding and empathy were missing in your response. Here's the thing, it's easier to keep doing things the same old way than to hold yourself accountable to putting in the effort to be a better listener.

You might not have become a good listener because you just are on autopilot, exhausted, and overwhelmed with all the roles you play. This overwhelm leads you to only passively half-listening at home. Of course, you deserve to feel like your home is a sanctuary to relax and rejuvenate, but you don't want to be so relaxed and tuned out that you're a lazy listener for your partner. This will only lead you to more Argument Hangovers.

For you to become a good listener—wait, let's kick this up a notch—a *great* listener, it is required that you give your full attention and presence to your partner. No side conversations, no phone, and no working on something else when it comes to having these more important or emotional conversations. Listening is actually a very powerful action. Yes, you read that correctly. Listening is not something that happens passively like breathing; it is a conscious, deliberate action that is required to be an empowered couple!

There are many good things that happen passively, such as breathing, chewing and digesting your food, at times you even drive passively, but there are these major things you cannot do passively: listen, understand, and show love to your partner, especially in the middle of a conflict. It is critical to understand that *listening does not mean you'll always agree.* We repeat, listening does not guarantee you will agree with your partner. This should give you a sigh of relief because you don't have to let go of your perspective completely in order to make your partner feel understood. Listening empathetically does not mean that you give in or fold your own entire view.

This is counterintuitive because you want the conflict to be resolved by one of you finally agreeing with the other person, but this feeds into a destructive game of one person winning and one person losing. You may even catch yourself trying to argue and defend your point with more and more evidence because you want them to see it your way. Or worse, you diminish and disregard what your partner says because you think they don't have enough evidence for their argument.

But agreeing is not the goal during a conflict (or really when communicating any time). Instead, the goal is understanding each other. You might want to write this on your arm or somewhere visible to remember and master it: First seek to understand (through actual listening) before being understood. (A shout-out to Stephen Covey and his book *The 7 Habits of Highly Effective People* in which he said this![1])

When you listen to understand your partner, you're focused on:

- **Empathizing with their perspective.** Think about this for a second: do you want the person you love to be wrong just because they see things differently than you do? You two will always have two different realities because you're in two different bodies.
- **Validating their feelings.** You don't want to make your partner feel invalidated or diminished. You also don't want to get defensive because you don't think your actions warranted them to feel that way.
- **Making them feel safe to share.** If you repeatedly reject or deny what they say, you're not making them feel safe to open up to you. You want to make them feel like they're with a partner who loves them enough to listen even when you don't agree. For your partner, it's very healing to just be able to say what they feel without having to fight for why there's evidence for it.
- **Growing together as a couple.** Some of your best opportunities to grow as a person come from hearing your partner's perspective. You don't have to take it personally.
- **Showing that you love them.** Your partner doesn't really care about the flowers, gifts, and fancy date nights;

---

1 Covey, Stephen. *The 7 Habits of Highly Effective People.* Rev. Ed. New York: Free Press, 2004.

especially if they don't get to feel understood in the relationship. You could actually say that the quality of your love is shown through the way you listen. Love = listening.

When you are listening, you are *not*:

- Trying to identify where there are holes or missing logic in their statements.
- Trying to solve or fix it and tell them that they shouldn't have a problem because of x, y, and z.
- Telling them that it's not that big of a deal.
- Getting defensive and making what they say about you.
- Giving additional meaning to or misinterpreting what was actually said.

When you're truly listening, you're being a partner who sees that you can create even better solutions and ideas when you're both understood. In fact, a lot of times you two may be missing out on amazing possibilities because you're reacting to each other and not listening. If you just seek to understand each other, you can create a resourceful, powerful, and creative place to find win-win solutions. But only after you both can say "I feel understood."

Far too often, we fall into the trap of trying to solve the problem so that our partner feels better, when really your partner just wants their feelings and perspective to be validated first.

Then problem solving can commence. For example, we encountered a really tough few weeks three years back. Here's what happened: A family friend was over at our house for a nice evening together with a small group. They happened to ask a very common question: "So, when are you having kids?" Aaron quickly responded with, "Oh, no, I don't want kids!" Now, here's the thing. We had talked about our family plans many times before this and were on the same page. We had not decided if we wanted children yet, but were staying open to the idea, so when Aaron responded so quickly and seemingly definitively, it subtly hurt my feelings. Aaron didn't notice it right away, but over the next few days I was really short-tempered, distant, and wanted space from him. He didn't know why because we work together full time and normally enjoy being around each other 24/7. He felt like something was off but couldn't pinpoint why because that remark to the family friend didn't really stand out in his memory.

I finally told Aaron, "I know that we both don't want to have children right now, but I was subconsciously hurt by how you said it the other night. A fear came up for me that you wouldn't want to be with me if I did get pregnant unexpectedly. A part of me just wants to know that you'll be with me even if that happens." Now, Aaron could have responded with things like "Oh, that's not what I meant. You misinterpreted what I said" or "Did I say I would leave if you got pregnant? No, I didn't." In fact, even if he just said "I'm sorry" I wouldn't have really felt understood. Instead, he said "I can totally see why it could feel that way. Tell me a little more about your fear." His response made me feel safe to share my fear, validated, and that he empathized with my reality in that moment. It was an extremely healing and powerful moment that could have had many different realities if he chose to respond a different way.

In your own life, where have you missed out on opportunities to connect deeper, to learn more about each other's fears, and strengthen your bond because you weren't willing to understand your partner? Just take a moment to reflect on even recent events where you can now see you would have responded differently. The goal of this communication tool isn't that you'll be a perfect human being who never gets triggered. Instead, it's being more present and conscientious during your conversations, especially when it's about something important to one or both of you. Aim to listen to your partner to understand their reality, and empathize with how they feel! Set aside your need to either agree or disagree with them. If it feels difficult at first, which is natural, still try to imagine being in their shoes. Try to put yourself into their reality and what the situation or circumstance was like for them. Ask yourself *from their perspective, what must it be like for them? If I were in their shoes, what might it feel like?* Seeing it from their perspective doesn't invalidate yours; we promise. You *both* have a valid perspective.

Something profound can happen for your partner when they truly are understood: they feel seen. When they are seen, their original upset can even disappear. We watch couples practice the art of understanding each other, and the person that was originally upset usually ends up saying "I actually feel better. I don't even need a solution or an apology. I just feel great that I can tell you actually understand me." That level of listening is true love. Aim for that!

Now, a common concern we hear is that if they focus on being a better listener, they won't get a chance to share their perspective. That's a valid fear and exactly what leads to the next communication skill the two of you can implement during a conflict.

DESIGNATE PLAYING THE SPEAKER AND LISTENER ROLES

The moment you can tell emotions are starting to escalate and you are leaning toward interrupting each other and reacting (aka not listening), pause and do this: Designate who is the speaker and who is the listener for a certain period of time. For example, you'd say "Hey, it seems like our emotions are getting escalated and we aren't really listening to each other anymore. How about you be the speaker for the next three minutes, and I'll be the listener? Then we'll switch."

This simple strategy does a few things: it ensures you both get equal amounts of time to share, it forces the listener to pay attention without jumping in to respond, and it helps de-escalate rising emotions that come up between you two. As you learned earlier about

1. Designate the speaker & listener
2. Then switch

speaker   **listener**

creating agreements, the listener role is committing to not interrupting the speaker. We know that isn't easy, especially if your partner says something that you really want to respond to, but it's critical that you continue to just listen, and listen to *understand*. This means validating their perspective. There is no right/wrong or true/false because in this moment that is just what is true for them (as well as for you). So, each perspective is "right" because that is how it currently is. The listener can't put on reactive facial expressions, roll their eyes, or make gestures that are implying judgement. On the other side of things, the speaker must also keep the agreements set beforehand and commit to no yelling and no name calling, plus any other agreements you two chose to set.

When you two first implement this tool, make sure you set a specific amount of time for each person until you can reliably self-monitor. Depending on the topic and the level of emotions you two are feeling, start with one, three, or five minutes. It can be helpful to start with shorter increments of time, like one minute, so that the listener can really capture the essence of what the speaker is sharing. You can then go back and forth until you reach a point where you both are understood. So, it could be partner 1 for five minutes, partner 2 for five minutes, then back to partner 1 for three minutes, then partner 2 for three minutes. This is important because it also encourages even a more reserved partner to share themselves during their time. They can't just say "I don't want to talk" and shut down the conversation (except of course when a time-out is agreed upon). Ideally even a more reserved person would feel safe to share if they knew their partner was playing the listener role and going to let them finish their thought without being interrupted or invalidated. Don't worry, we'll go much more into communication differences with a reserved partner versus an assertive partner on page 154.

Let's recap before we go on to the next communication tool to use during conflict:

- Self-awareness is key (body language, how you're feeling, etc.).
- Identify if/when a time-out is needed.
- Designate one person as the speaker and one as the listener.
- Listen to your partner to understand, not to agree or disagree.

This next section will empower you, when you are playing the speaker role during a conflict, to share yourself in a non-combative way.

Just like it's not easy to be a great listener, it's not easy to be a constructive and effective speaker in times of high emotion. You can easily find yourself saying things you don't mean or pointing blame at your partner when deep down you want your conversation to lead to more love, not less. With each statement that you make during a fight, you're either building up toward a healthy resolution or a gnarly Argument Hangover. You're obviously reading this book to avoid that hangover and disconnection to truly be an empowered couple.

The difference between constructive and destructive language is subtle, and the easiest way to go from destructive to constructive is by switching "you" statements to "I" and "we" statements. "You" statements point blame, avoid taking responsibility, and likely put your partner on the defensive. They are destructive more often than not. "I" and "we" statements come from a place of self-awareness, personal responsibility, being on the same side, and tend to be more constructive.

"You" statements	"I" statements	"We" statements
"You never say thank you, and you totally take me for granted."	"What's coming up for me is this fear that I am taken for granted."	"I think we could both work on showing each other more appreciation."
"You never make time for me! I told you that I feel neglected and you haven't done anything about it!"	"I just started to realize that I'd like to have more quality time together where we aren't distracted."	"What if we explored different creative ways we can schedule date nights and get more quality time together?"
"You are spending way too much money and completely disregarding the budget we set up."	"I'm committed to us both feeling more financial freedom, and it'd mean a lot to me if we reviewed the budget we set up."	"It seems to me like maybe we've been off track with our financial goals and plan."

As you can see from the table, it's a subtle change in language that can make all the difference. Here are some prompts for how you can communicate from an "I" and "we" perspective:

- What's coming up for me is _____
- What I am committed to is _____
- I just started to realize _____
- We can work on _____

- It seems like we _____
- What if we brought more attention to _____?

These prompts are based on personal responsibility, the commitment to being on the same team, and the aim to be intentional and constructive. As opposed to "you" statements that sound like:

- If only you would _____
- You never _____
- You always _____
- You made me feel _____

These "you" statements are based on blame, pointing the finger, deflecting personal responsibility, and are more destructive and will

you two vs the problem

the problem

you two vs each other

likely lead to your partner getting defensive. When you focus on the "I" and "we" statements, you are showing that you're standing beside your partner and looking at the challenge as opposed to "you" statements that stand against your partner in battle.

It's easy to forget that the person you love is your partner when you are really attached to your perspective being right and theirs being wrong. If you think about it, you're wasting precious energy fighting against them, rather than making the "problem" the thing you attack together. The problem is just an opportunity to discover a solution as a team. Make the problem what you fight against, not each other. One of the best ways to ensure this is by designating "speaker" and "listener" roles so you each get to share and be understood.

It's not always easy to be a great listener, but it can also be quite challenging at first to shift into being an effective speaker/communicator. Putting that into perspective, they're both much easier than continuing to take things personally, fighting against each other, withholding communication, building up resentment, and prolonging your Argument Hangovers, wouldn't you say? There are some people in the relationship space that say "active listening" is unrealistic and too difficult for couples to maintain for any real length of time. We want to take a moment to address this idea. Human beings have the most sophisticated neurological system on the planet. You can create your own memories and paint a picture of the future life you want to live, use all your faculties to invent new things, and live in the most abundant and technologically connected society that has ever lived! How can it be "too hard" for one of you to listen to your loving partner, repeat what you heard them say so they feel understood, then switch roles so that you both feel connected and on the same page? We've received hundreds of messages from couples who practice these principles and say "we've never been more connected and on the same page" because they're finally listening to understand, and you can, too! This is an aspirational book and we choose to see you for your unlimited potential and all that you can become together. We know you can incorporate this simple habit for the sake of reducing your Argument Hangovers and being an empowered couple that is an example to all around you. This leads us to the next tool for fighting smarter during conflicts and shortening the Argument Hangover.

BECOME A CRYSTAL-CLEAR COMMUNICATOR

To say it simply, you're probably not being as clear when you speak as you think you are. It can be so frustrating when you've said how you feel and what you need repeatedly, and your partner isn't getting it. You can feel like you're speaking different languages and even make remarks like "I said it in plain English, I don't understand what isn't clear for you" or "I told you what I wanted last week, so you should know." In a way, you are speaking different languages and that's why your partner doesn't understand you. In your mind, you know exactly what you mean. But you aren't being as effective in making your thoughts and feelings clearly known and transmitted to your partner. You can both hear the word "romance" or "quality time" and you'll each imagine different things—a different meaning for the same word. You might simply say "please take out the trash" and for you that means in the next five minutes, but for your partner that means sometime in the next twenty-four hours—two different meanings. So while you might feel like you're both speaking English, you might as well be speaking Spanish because every word has a different meaning for each of you. What's the bottom line here? Even if you think you are being clear, if you keep having to repeat yourself, you might need to look at how you are communicating (assuming your partner is also listening, of course). As an example, here are some common conversations we hear with couples we coach:

The topic of conversation	What "partner 1" means	What "partner 2" means
P1: "I want our intimacy to improve. I don't think we have that spark anymore." P2: "I don't know why you could feel that way, we went on a date and had sex last night."	"Intimacy to me is having a meaningful conversation without distractions. Making eye contact, talking about our emotions, asking each other great questions. Intimacy is an emotional connection to me."	"Intimacy to me is having sex 3 to 4 times per week, great kisses, and snuggling at night before bed."
P1: "I need you to help around the house more. I'm overwhelmed." P2: "I'm trying to help. I cleaned the garage and took out the trash today."	"Helping around the house means cleaning the dishes after we eat, taking out the bathroom trash when you see it full, picking up your coffee cup after you drink it in your office and wiping your pee off the toilet seat."	P2: "I'm doing what I know to do. I'm not as great at anticipating what else might need to be done."

In our coaching sessions we'll watch the frustration build as one person feels like they've said the same thing for months and nothing has changed. We'll intercept the conversation to work with that person. The speaker is usually surprised to get the feedback that what they're saying isn't actually all that clear. This is typically because they are making one of the following common mistakes:

- Speaking in absolutes. ("You always . . . " or "You never . . . ")
- Being vague. ("I want more quality time" or "I need more help")
- Externally pointing the finger or blaming instead of saying what you actually need. ("See, that husband still finds his wife attractive")
- Being passive aggressive. ("No, I'll take care of it. It's not like I'm tired or anything")
- Being sarcastic. ("Maybe you'll remember our anniversary this year")

- Making exaggerations/rude statements. ("You're always nagging me")

The person we are working with is usually convinced that their partner should know exactly what they mean. This falls into the deadly idea of "they should just know," which plagues many relationships. No, your partner shouldn't just know! Your partner cannot read your mind, and they can only make assumptions based on their interpretations of the information they are given.

What if we told you to make us some cookies and that's all we said? With that little information, you can only assume based on your experience and what cookies mean to you. If you think of chocolate chip cookies, that's what you'd make. But you don't know that when we say cookies (since we are allergic to chocolate, gluten, and dairy), we actually mean to make gluten-free, vegan, oatmeal raisin cookies. And we meant in the next hour, for a group of friends that we have coming over. So, neither one of us are going to be set up for success here, to say the least.

You can read this and think *duh*. But those are the kind of gross assumptions you make about each other when you two aren't clear in your communication. Of course, assuming what type of cookies someone wants isn't life altering, but it is when it's something really important to your partner. Over time, you can start to feel that your partner isn't meeting your needs, which for some means ending the relationship. But what if they aren't meeting your needs because they don't *really* know what you need? That's good news because you two can now work on being clearer with what you say to each other. You want to be more detailed than you think is necessary. At first it might feel like overkill, but it needs to be until you're more on the same page by being better communicators. This is how detailed you want to be:

Vague Communication	Clear Communication
"I'm not sure if you still find me attractive."	"I'm feeling a little self-conscious right now and could use some extra compliments in the morning, and maybe you could pat my butt as you walk by, and caress my body as we make love."
"We need to be more aware of our financial spending."	"I'm feeling a bit stressed in this area, so let's work together each week to lower spending for the next six months. I'm committed to paying off all debt and feeling more freedom. Can we both agree to talk to each other about any purchases over $100? And we each get $200 of fun money per month."

Let's break down some elements of being more clear in what you say to your partner:

- **Give them more context.** This can be how you are feeling, background details, or why it's important to you. Without this, they might not realize where you're coming from.
- **Say what your positive commitment is.** Behind every statement is some kind of commitment. Are you committed to being more connected, having more freedom, or more love? This sets a positive tone for the details you'll provide.
- **Give specific details.** This can include the specific time frame, what it looks like for you, and what the words really mean to you. Don't just say "more quality time," say how much time, how often, doing what, who's around, what you are doing, etc.
- **Get their acknowledgement.** Ask them if what you said is clear. If you aren't sure it was clear enough, ask them to either repeat back what they heard, or simply ask "does that feel clear to you or should I provide more detail?"

As you attempt to be more clear, you are adding this additional detail to make sure you two are on the same page because while you both might be speaking the same language, you can have very different interpretations of each other's words. You might be thinking *well, what do we do then if words mean different things to each of us? Does one person have to sacrifice their meaning for the other person's?*

Absolutely not, that is limited thinking and we don't believe in the word "sacrifice" in relationships. We believe in win-win solutions! If one person has to sacrifice something, you didn't spend enough time getting creative and understanding each other. You likely spent your precious energy arguing between one opinion/solution versus another, which is only two out of the 100+ solutions that exist if you were open to exploring them. There *is* a win-win solution for both the small things and big things in your relationship. But to find these win-win solutions, you have to first be clear in your communication to stay on the same team.

If you two are intentional about becoming better listeners and clearer speakers, you will be able to blast through any challenge that comes up. Every word you speak matters. Slow down and focus on being more detailed and purposeful with what you say. Don't clutter the conversation by saying things you don't really mean because of the emotions you're feeling, and don't assume your partner "should" know what you mean with vague statements. You can feel the emotions and still choose your words. The alternative is that you just let yourself have a free-for-all as the speaker and you create more damage than the original cause of the disagreement. But that's not what you want, hence why you've chosen to read this book and practice these tools.

TIME TO TAKE THE LEAD

As you're reading this chapter, you're in one of three places:

1. Your partner is reading the book with you and implementing the tools.
2. Your partner is reading the book with you but is not implementing the tools with you.
3. Your partner has not started to read the book with you (yet)!

Wherever you fall, we encourage you to take the lead on implementing these tools the next time a disagreement arises so that you can shorten or avoid the Argument Hangover. We know you can read that and think *shoot, am I going to have to be the one that takes the lead while my partner can just stay the same?* We get it. But, yes, we do want to give you some tough love and encourage you to take the lead, shift the actions you take during conflict, and show your partner a new way to handle arguments. The ultimate goal, of course, is that you both implement these new relationship skills in the short-term and long-term. It often isn't sustainable if one person focuses on being constructive and the other let's themselves get away with the same destructive patterns. Your intention should be that over time, you are both initiating better communication habits. But that might take a different amount of time for both of you.

If you sometimes feel discouraged that you're the only one doing the work in the relationship, this next section will give you hope. And, will show that by you going first, it will positively influence your partner over some time. Have you ever heard of "mirror neurons?" A mirror neuron is a distinct type of neuron in our brain that allows us to learn through observation and imitation. A team of Italian researchers discovered mirror neurons in the 1990s when they were studying the behavior of monkeys.[2] To put it simply, their research found that mirror neurons fired in one subject when they observed another subject take an action. So, what does this have to do with fighting smarter with your partner? You could say that as you implement these healthy skills, your partner's brain will fire similar neural pathways and learn through observation. There's still more research to be done about mirror neurons, but we're excited by the possibility that your partner could start to imitate your behaviors!

---

2 Di Pellegrino, G., L. Fadiga, L. Fogassi, V. Gallese, and G. Rizzolatti. 1992. "Understanding motor events, a neurophysiological study." *Exp. Brain Res.* 91:176–180.

It might not happen overnight, but what if you stayed consistent with listening to understand when you'd normally interrupt? What if you started sentences in a disagreement with "what's coming up for me is . . ." instead of "you are causing me to . . . "? Your partner will notice that, even if subconsciously, and begin to mirror your behaviors and actions during arguments. They might not even consciously know it's happening, but their brain will be firing and assimilating through your example and leadership.

Reading this should excite you, and also invite you to step up into your personal leadership! By no means do you have to step up alone forever, but you are modeling the example of what it means to be unconditional toward your partner. Unfortunately, what happens in many relationships is that when one person isn't stepping up to put in equal effort, the other person starts to put in less effort as well. This creates a destructive cycle because both people are then waiting for the other person to do something before they do. You might have seen social media quotes that say "a relationship is 50/50" but that is not the right mindset. If one partner starts to put in 40 percent, the other person may start to go down to 40 percent effort, and on and on. Your actions can't be conditional based on what your partner is doing. You should commit yourself to putting in 100 percent effort to use these healthy communication and conflict resolution skills. Remember that when you lead by example, your partner will begin to mirror the same. It's science!

Now that you are prepared with during-conflict skills, the next chapter will go into how to fully resolve a disagreement, find more creative solutions, and completely end the Argument Hangover period.

YOUR GAME PLAN

- Be more self-aware: take a breath and slow down during the conflict and be conscientious of your tone of voice, body language, and the words you are using.
- Identify and request a "time-out" if needed.
- Designate one person as the speaker and one as the listener.
- Listen to your partner to understand, not to agree or disagree.
- When speaking, focus on being clearer, and get acknowledgement from them that you both mean the same thing.

You can shorten the Argument Hangover by learning to be better listeners, clearer speakers, and focusing on understanding even if you don't agree.

7

AFTER CONFLICT

"There can be no deep disappointment where there is not deep love."

—Martin Luther King Jr.

Regarding your relationship, would you agree or disagree with the following statement? "At times I feel our disagreements never get resolved." Well, when we asked that question to the 78 couples who took the P/E assessment, on the same scale of 1–5 from strongly disagree to strongly agree, the majority selected 4 = Agree to that same statement. And not only that, but when we host our in-person couples workshops, 90 percent or more of their hands go up when we ask the question "Who feels like it's those same two or three recurring disagreements that keep coming up over and over again?" They raise their hands without hesitating because it's usually just a few disagreements that keep coming up. These disagreements never really got fully complete and are lingering around to easily get triggered in a future moment.

Why the Argument Hangover feels so horrible and lingers for hours, days, or even years is because you're lacking the post-conflict tools to fully complete conflicts emotionally. Even when you have mastered the listening skills to understand each other during a conflict, it does not guarantee a full completion of a conflict. Interesting, right? If you implement what you learned in the before and during conflict stages, the steps outlined in this chapter won't be as severe or lengthy. You will be able to more quickly resolve conflicts and come up with creative solutions together.

No matter how big or small your disagreement feels to you, just saying "I'm sorry" rarely does the job to make your partner feel like it's resolved. Even if one of you says I'm sorry, you can still feel the lingering sadness or pain from how the disagreement went (hence, you're having an Argument Hangover). We're not saying that you shouldn't apologize to each other; we're just saying that it's only *one* of the ingredients to actually closing out the conflict emotionally. Think of it like a circle. When you only say "I'm sorry," it leaves part of the circle open, which increases the likelihood that you will carry unresolved emotion, that the same argument will come up again, or that it will build into long-term resentment.

"I'm sorry" doesn't quite close the circle

Here are some common signs that your "conflict circles" are not getting fully closed, which shows that "I'm sorry" isn't going to cut it.

- One or both of you still needs a lot of space from each other.

- You continue to bring up the past in disagreements saying things like "This is exactly what happened a month ago."
- You find yourself keeping an internal tally or score of all the times your partner frustrates you.
- You still feel tension and on edge, like you have to "walk on eggshells" to keep from triggering a fight.
- You don't trust their "I'm sorry" to mean that anything will actually change.
- The same disagreement keeps coming up over and over.

Since the goal of this entire book is to empower you with skills to shorten the Argument Hangover period, the actions you take in the post-conflict phase are critical. How long you wait to implement these steps dictates how long you both can feel disconnected, hurt, or resentful. As we mentioned earlier in the book, some couples don't "close the conflict" even years later and basically become numb and resigned in the relationship. As you read and implement these next skills, your focus is to initiate them faster and faster to minimize Argument Hangovers and maximize connection on the other side of conflict.

The question you want to ask yourself is "How much life am I willing to lose from the Argument Hangover period?" That might sound like a dramatic question, but it's true. When your Argument Hangover lingers, you're missing out on love, fun together, and the joy of life. We aren't on this planet forever, so how long are you willing to let it go on? Our personal marriage goal, and what we encourage for all couples, is to fight smarter and to initiate the after-conflict closure within minutes instead of hours, days, or years. Imagine only being disconnected for five minutes. Wouldn't that be powerful for your relationship? It's completely possible for you.

THE 5 R'S TO REPAIRING AFTER A CONFLICT

So, how do you "close the circle" and fully resolve these conflicts? We've organized this process into the 5 R's to repairing after a conflict:

reflect + responsibility + remind + reconnect + reconcile. It's helpful to follow through these steps in order, but it doesn't always have to go in a linear way. The important part is that you cover all of them. Sometimes these 5 R's can occur while you're still in the original disagreement, or after you took a "time-out" and have come back after.

Step #1: Reflect

It's important that both of you expand your ability to reflect internally at what lessons might be there for you. Even if you initially think the disagreement was caused by your partner, there is something for you to realize about yourself. Remember that your relationship is the greatest opportunity to grow as a person because it is a reflection of you—like an orange has orange juice inside, what came out of you was already there, not created by an external action of your partner. You don't want to miss out on a golden opportunity to become an even better person and partner because you're unwilling to look internally, do you?

Here's the thing: you've got to face the junk inside, which can be any stored up, suppressed, or locked away emotions from your past. It's okay, we all have limitations/barriers to how much love, kindness, compassion, joy, energy, or enthusiasm we allow ourselves to express and to receive inside. These limitations can be from withheld, suppressed, and unconscious doubt, fear, unworthiness, judgement, shame, hate, anger, sadness, or hurt. They can only be transformed by shedding light on them from our own personal reflections.

Without reflecting, you can miss out on discovering what you really feel, need, or desire in the relationship. For example, some people will try to finish conversations by saying "I'm sorry, I just had a really tough day and I'm tired." Sure, there might be times that you were particularly sensitive because of your day, or even that you didn't take care of yourself and you're "hangry" (hungry + angry). If that's the case, you still want to reflect on how things like that contributed to the disagreement with your partner. But many times couples stop once they find a surface level cause and don't look deeper.

Maybe something got triggered in you and this disagreement is an opportunity to heal something inside of yourself that happened in this relationship or in a past relationship. For example, Jocelyn told her story about feeling men were cheaters and she didn't trust them. This created a type of wound within herself. But rather than carry that with her the rest of her life, she used this reflection time after conflicts with me (Aaron) to heal from those past hurts. Now she is able to trust and love more fully!

Each disagreement will require a different amount of reflection time. Sometimes in only five minutes you can discover something, but for deeper hurts and lessons, you might be personally reflecting over a period of a few months. This is how you evolve into becoming the best version of yourself. Here are some questions you can ask yourself in this reflection time:

- Why did I get so triggered in this conversation?
- What is really the root cause of my frustration?
- Is there something I need that's been suppressed and I haven't vocalized?
- What exactly upset me about what they said?
- Do I have an unmet expectation?
- Is there something for me to heal within this relationship?
- Is there something for me to heal from past relationships?
- Was my reaction due to the topic at hand, or is it really from something else I haven't talked about?
- What is my fear in the relationship?
- What is the true desire that is missing for me?

As you two master the skills in this book, you'll eventually get to the point where you two can ask each other these questions toward the end of a conflict to help each other reflect. You'll know you're mastering these principles when you get to the point where you know your partner's actions aren't about you, but something inside of them, and vice versa. You'll be able to get curious about yourself and your partner for what healing and lesson is available to you at that moment. But until you feel ready to ask each other these reflective questions, give yourself some time to either journal or walk to think about them on your own. Once you have reflected and discovered something about yourself, you can then move to the next of the 5 R's.

Step #2: Responsibility

When you first read the word "responsibility," do you think of obligation, burden, or blaming yourself? Or that it means you're in the wrong? That's not what we mean by taking responsibility in this context. Taking responsibility for a conflict isn't easy because, frankly, we live in a culture that is quick to place blame. We've been conditioned to think that responsibility is bad because it gets us into trouble or signifies we are at fault. It's easier to blame it on your employer, your parents, the government, the economy, your busy schedule, and even on your partner. We're not pointing fingers at you. It's this dang thing called an ego! As a human, our ego tries to protect itself by shifting blame to someone/something else. We've caught ourselves saying things like "I wouldn't have gotten so mad if you didn't talk to me that way" or "I wouldn't have cursed if you didn't push my buttons." These are examples of "deflecting" which is an ego defense mechanism to make you feel better about yourself in the moment and to avoid responsibility.

Truthfully, the only reason we can write this book is because we've caught these dynamics in our own relationship, as well as the couples we've worked with. Of the 5 R's to repair from a conflict, this has been the hardest one for us to master, and tends to be the hardest one for most couples. Believe it or not, it's one of the most critical parts for you both to be able to forgive, heal, and fully recover from the Argument Hangover. If you find that your partner seems to be holding on to some resentment from a conflict, it's likely because this responsibility step has not been taken.

Warning: though this may be the case for your partner, you cannot just come out and say to them, "Hey, you need to take responsibility," especially if they are still in the triggered emotion. This also cannot be a drive-by conversation you have with them, as it will just trigger them more. In the beginning of this step, you will need to have agreements set up and ask for permission to coach or give feedback to each other. These conversations on responsibility will need to occur within a structured time, with no distractions, and in a calm and connected state.

> It's important to understand that your brain is there for you to survive, and that includes creating ways to protect yourself from being wrong or invalidated.

Taking it a step further, the brain will even find evidence for why it was your partner's fault and not yours. You might have gone to your partner and said "I'm sorry, that was my fault" when you finally realize that you were the one that instigated it. And that's great, but can you take responsibility even when you don't think you should? Can you take responsibility when you feel you were an innocent bystander just reacting to the circumstances?

Level one mastery of this step would look like taking responsibility when you are aware you caused the conflict. Level two mastery is when you're willing to take responsibility regardless of who caused the conflict, to look for what there is that you can take ownership for. Since there were two people in that conversation, one of them was you! So what role did you play in escalating or keeping that argument going? What role "didn't you play" to keep you both on the same side looking at the challenge together? You might be thinking *why would I take the blame if this whole thing was because they (fill in the blank)?* Again, taking responsibility isn't placing blame. In fact, let's just say self-blame or blaming them is so outdated, old news, and a little childish. You're better than that now, friends. We say that responsibility = response-ability. It's your ability to respond consciously in any given situation.

Whoa, let that definition sink in. Taking responsibility is when you take ownership for what you can do and the fact that you have the ability to respond in a way that empowers you, and serves the betterment of your relationship regardless of circumstances. Basically, you're saying "I see my part in this." Even actively looking for it, not because you were wrong, but because you want to grow and be the best partner you can be! Here are some examples that show the difference between deflecting responsibility and taking responsibility (response-ability):

Deflecting Responsibility	Taking Response-ability
P1: "I wouldn't have gotten so short with you if you weren't nagging on me after a long day." P2: "You put me in this position because you didn't ask if I needed help."	P1: "I can see now that I didn't tell you I had a rough day and that I needed a few minutes of quiet, alone time. I left you in the dark and just reacted rudely." P2: "I can see now that I wasn't up front about all the things I needed help with or seeing when a good time might be for you to talk."
P1: "I had to leave the room because you kept interrupting me." P2: "Well you weren't listening to me, so I had to keep repeating myself."	P1: "I shouldn't have just left the room and left you wondering when I'd be back. I could have chosen differently." P2: "I can see now that I talked over you and didn't keep our agreements because I was triggered. I didn't give you a chance to share your side of things."

In these examples, it doesn't matter who "caused it." Both people can take response-ability for their side of things. You control how you respond. But if you only say "I'm sorry," you're not taking responsibility and it wouldn't necessarily resolve the conflict emotionally. That's why you hear your partner say things like "this is exactly like last time!" Because it wasn't complete for them, they didn't feel like you acknowledged your part, didn't see your desire to act as a team, or didn't think you recognized the impact that your actions had. Even if your intentions were good, guess what? They can still have a negative impact on your partner. Taking responsibility is acknowledging that you chose to take or not take a certain action, and realizing how to avoid this in the future. You might think you'll feel better about yourself if you deflect the blame on to your partner, but in the long-run, you will feel like a more powerful person when you take response-ability for whatever your part was. Once you two have taken some time to reflect, and you each shared your response-ability, you can go into the third R to repair after a conflict.

Step #3: Remind
Earlier in the book we talked about the power of creating agreements/ground rules for times of conflict. As we said, you won't be perfect at keeping the agreements until they become so ingrained that they're your natural habits. But if you just ignore that you broke an agreement, you won't fully recover from the Argument Hangover. When you are not consistent or committed to keeping the agreements, you lose trust with your partner and yourself. This is because you are not honoring your word to what you promised. This is a lack of integrity in the things you say and what you give your word to. When this happens repeatedly, how can anyone ever trust what you say, how can anyone ever trust you? (The answer is they can't.)

So, as a couple, you want to review and remind each other of the agreements after the fight. Don't say "you broke this" or "I broke that." Instead, review them like this:

1. Pull out your written agreements/ground rules for times of conflict.

2. Review each one and ask yourselves, "How did we do in keeping this agreement?"

3. Keep the language focused on "we" so that you're accountable as a team.

4. If you notice that you were the one to break the agreement, you can take responsibility for it by saying "I broke the agreement not to leave the room. For that I am sorry." You also want to acknowledge any emotional impact that action had on your partner.

5. Once you've reviewed them to see which ones you kept and broke, you both want to recommit to implementing and honoring them.

The final step is critical. Just like creating the agreements in the first place, you must give your word to them again. You can't do this just to appease your partner and to move on from the argument. You do this because it puts you back into a powerful place where you're committing to agreements again. You can only get better at keeping them if you're accountable and you've got your promise behind them. Without this step, your partner can fear that these patterns will just keep happening over and over again because you're not willing to commit to them. Your word starts to mean less and less.

Be careful not to skip over the agreements that seem less important only to you, like shutting down and getting quiet. Just because it might not seem as obviously painful or hurtful as cursing, slamming doors, or name calling doesn't mean that shutting down isn't hurtful to your partner. Make sure that you remind each other and recommit to even these types of agreements so that you both stay in the conversation during times of conflict.

There may be times when you come together and realize that agreements you made with each other before are not the ones that will be the most impactful moving forward. You may have noticed that there are different actions now that are triggering you, so you can make new agreements that will better serve you both. Once you two have reminded each other of the agreements (or remade them) and recommitted to them, the next of the 5 R's naturally unfolds.

Step #4: Reconnect

After a disagreement, it can feel like the last thing you want is to hug, kiss, or even make love. You might even try to distract yourself from the frustration by moving on to chores, work, or playing with the kids. After a fight, you can feel kind of wounded and vulnerable, so you can think that physical space is the best option to recover. You are in the Argument Hangover!

But it's critical that you reconnect physically as soon as possible. And yes, even before you feel like it. It can seem like you should wait till you feel "ready," but taking the action to be affectionate stimulates those feel-good hormones in your body. Really, try it. This is what is called "breaking the physical touch barrier." Even if you're still sad or mad, a hug reminds you that you love each other and likely will cause those negative feelings to lessen. Immediately you have that feeling of being partners, on the same team, and fundamentally committed to each other. Your body actually releases those "happy chemicals" automatically. It really is an amazing and magical feeling that happens in milliseconds. This is another area for you to step up and lead in the relationship. Be a partner that is willing to go first and initiate reconciliation through a simple touch! Think of it as you have a "magic touch" if you want, because it will feel like that to your partner!

Unfortunately, we have heard far too many couples say that they haven't been sexually intimate for a week, two weeks, or even months because they're still upset with each other. They're waiting till they "feel like it" to initiate that sexual connection, but this just perpetuates the disconnection cycle. While it seems counterintuitive, we actually suggest that you initiate sexual intimacy as soon as possible after a disagreement. Not because of the cliché idea of "make-up sex," but because of how it brings you back together and makes you both feel united. If you don't feel quite ready to be sexually intimate, make sure you at least give each other a strong hug and maybe even a smooch. Hug them before you feel ready because they're your partner, and you're a team working toward "fighting smarter."

The mind-body connection is strong. While thoughts can change quickly, emotion is slow to shift. The biochemistry takes time to turn with thought but they are always tied together. There is a lag period for emotion to match your thoughts, so if you make your body take an action toward connecting, your thoughts will follow, causing the emotion to get on board.

Step #5: Reconcile

Now gets to the part that many of you were waiting for . . . the solution. Once you have reflected, taken responsibility, reminded each other of the agreements, and physically reconnected, you then want to reconcile your options and create a win-win solution. Far too many people try to jump the solution before any of the other steps and it doesn't go well. In fact, when we talk to most women they don't even want to hear solutions until the other steps are covered. We don't love gender norms, but we do talk to a *lot* of couples and have noticed that men tend to be "fixers" and feel that if they present a solution it will end the disagreement. But we put "reconcile" as the last step here because things usually get repaired easier when each of your feelings has been acknowledged in the previous steps first.

If the argument contained a lot of bickering over who's opinion or solution was better, you likely didn't get to something that felt like a win-win scenario. Maybe one of you just wanted the disagreement to end so you threw up your hands and said "whatever you want" even though you really didn't feel like that included what matters to you. When you're both ready to reconcile the options, you want to do the following:

1. Clearly write out your goal or what you two are hoping for from the solution. This comes from the discovery of what you do want from the conflict rather than focusing on what you don't want. For example: that we both feel we're getting quality time, or that we have a financial plan that allows us to both feel free and secure.

2. Write out 10 different solutions or options that support the goal you both share. Note that it doesn't say two options, which is where most couples find themselves: arguing one opinion versus the other. There are many more solutions/options that you just haven't taken the time to think of together.

3. Talk through which option (or options) feels like a win-win to you both.

4. Try implementing and taking action on one solution.

If you feel like there isn't a win-win option, you're either too attached to your perspective or you're not being creative enough as a couple. There *is* a win-win solution for you as a team. Sure, it might take one or both of you adjusting your perspective slightly, but that's why you want to spend plenty of time hearing out each other's solutions, because you could be misinterpreting them. You two need to think outside the box because there's likely an option that neither of you have thought of yet. In the process of writing the 10 possible options, you will find that you can easily get to 3 or 4 logical ones. Let yourself have fun and write options that may not even be rational or practical for 5–7. You will find yourself laughing and getting more creative. For options 8–10 you may discover new and different solutions that you never thought of before! When you are connected, creative, and having more fun, you think of options that you never would have on your own . . . that's called being an empowered couple! Here are a couple of examples of creating these solution lists:

Goal: We both get more quality time together **Challenge that led to conflict:** Difficulty getting a babysitter and a long to-do list
1. We put up a post on social media asking for referrals
2. We hire our neighbor's teenage kid twice per month
3. We turn off the TV an hour earlier to talk at night
4. We take the kids with us on the date once per week
5. We wake up an hour earlier than the kids to have coffee together
6. We totally abandon our current life and start new in Fiji (the fun, impractical idea)
7. We send the kids off to a boarding school for 3 months (the fun, irrational idea)
8. We quit our jobs, sell the house, and travel the country in an RV (the fun, irrational idea)
9. We ask our parents to move to our city to help out
10. We hire a house cleaner twice per month to cut down on the to-do list

Goal: We pay off all debt to experience more of the world together **Challenge that led to conflict:** Different spending habits, financial frustration. and no vacation for 2 years
1. We each get $150 of fun money per month and when it's gone, it's gone
2. One of us starts a side business to bring in an extra $500 per month
3. We sell one of our cars to pay off the debt, and share a car for 1 year
4. We hire a financial coach to help us create a better system
5. We go on a road trip for a week within the next 2 months instead of flying
6. We can rob a bank (the fun, irrational idea)
7. We can impersonate a celebrity couple and get our trip paid for (the fun, irrational idea)
8. We can rent out our second car through an app when we are not using it
9. We can sell items in the house that we haven't used in more than 1 year
10. We ask our bosses how we can add more value to justify a raise of $10,000 per year

As you read these examples, you might not love every solution upon first glance. When you're working with your partner on your solution list, don't judge or reject one because you don't like it. The goal is to keep the energy positive, creative, lighthearted, and forward moving. Hence why some of the irrational and impractical options are listed. Coming up with an option that makes you laugh together is a good thing! If you say things like "I definitely am not doing that" or "No, I don't like that one because . . . " then you start to dampen the mood and it doesn't feel like an enjoyable conversation between you two. The more open and creative you are, the better solutions you end up thinking of. You could even get to the point where you say, "Wow, that's such a great idea that we've never thought of before!"

Once you have reconciled the options and come up with the win-win solution, it's important you both agree on expectations regarding details and timing. Without that, one of you might think that you'll take action within twenty-four hours and the other one thinks it's within a month. You want to get on the same page for what the actions are and when they'll be taken. This part is important. It can be very frustrating if you come up with the win-win solution, but then neither of you follow through on it. You can even lose trust in each other if action isn't taken in the agreed upon timeframe. Make sure you two create calendar reminders or visual cues of your solution so it gets set into motion. Even if you try one of the solutions you agreed upon and it turns out that it didn't produce the outcome you were looking for, it's okay. You have a whole list of other options you can still try

As we said earlier, you don't have to necessarily do these 5 R steps in order, but you do want to cover all of them. You might also find that you complete three of the R's within an hour, but need a little more time to reflect and reconcile. That's okay, just make sure too much time doesn't pass before you complete them. Otherwise your busy life can take over, the conflict doesn't actually get repaired, then it gets triggered again in the near future—the circle might not be fully closed.

The main intention with these 5 steps is to recover from an Argument Hangover emotionally, because just saying "I'm sorry" doesn't necessarily do that. If you try to "move on" after a disagreement without completing the 5 R's, you'll keep having the same disagreements over and over again, and will likely encounter resentments toward each other. As you move into the next chapter, you will learn about each of your communication styles and how to give each other the required time to process your emotions.

5 R's to repair a conflict

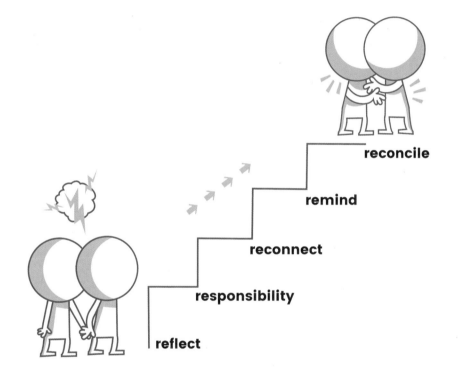

reconcile

remind

reconnect

responsibility

reflect

YOUR GAME PLAN

- Reflect on the lessons you can learn individually.
- Take responsibility and own the role you did play in the conflict.
- Reconnect by breaking the physical touch barrier.
- Remind each other of the agreements you made for times of conflict.
- Reconcile by creating multiple, creative win-win solutions and take action on one.

> You can shorten the Argument Hangover by implementing the 5 R's to repair after a conflict.

8

YOUR COMMUNICATION PERSONALITY TYPES

"Your partner may *never* communicate exactly like you, but you don't have to change them, just understand your type and dynamic."

—Aaron & Jocelyn Freeman

Did you know that each of us has a communication personality type? Everyone loves a good personality test, right? We have taken just about every single assessment out there to learn more about ourselves! It's empowering to learn more about your personal tendencies, what naturally drives and motivates you, and also where you could potentially grow. The thing is, all of those personality tests just focus on you as an individual and don't actually address the way it creates certain dynamics between you and a romantic partner.

You two can avoid the pains of the Argument Hangover by understanding more about your own communication personality type as well as your partner's. You don't need to change each other or get frustrated by how your partner communicates, which can be an underlying aggravator and instigator of conflict. In this chapter, you'll discover the main elements of what gives you a communication personality type, the most common dynamics that couples fall into, and how to better communicate with each other. And while we don't believe that you should change yourself to fit into a "type" that's unnatural or inauthentic, we will provide ways that you can grow or evolve to be an even better partner.

So, why is this so useful to know? In our work with couples, we're always documenting, collecting data, and researching trends. Jocelyn and I both come from research backgrounds, so we love to see how trends can be revealed for couples to better understand themselves and not feel alone in the challenges they face. We love when couples take a sigh of relief and say "oh, it's not just us," as they hear many other couples experience the same challenges communicating because of their differences.

After synthesizing thousands of conversations, we made a striking observation that two people could encounter recurring communication frustrations even when they have so much compatibility and have deep love for reach other. For many couples, their different personalities (which include communication styles) was part of what attracted them to each other in the first place, but at some point, became a source of frustration, tension, and unresolved issues. Think of those moments when you let out a sound of frustration because your partner's communication habits are different than yours. Funny how something that connects you can also be something that disconnects you, isn't it? You could even learn the most effective relationship skills from any expert but still be unable to make them work within the context of your own relationship if you believe your partner is implementing them the wrong way (too slow, too forcefully, or just not how you would do it).

A quick and funny story about us. Early on in our partnership, Jocelyn would share all of her feelings quickly (imagine ten minutes' worth of talking crammed into three minutes), then pause. I (Aaron) would be silent for about five seconds, and she'd say "hello?" I'd say "what, I'm thinking." She'd say "still? I stopped talking a while ago." Then. I would snap back quickly, saying "stop rushing me, can't I get a second to think and even breathe?" This pattern of frustration would show up about twice per week. We didn't understand each other's communication styles, which was part of what inspired us to dive into this work and make it available for other couples. Imagine being able to see your similarities and differences as the ingredients that make you such a strong team!

DISCOVERING YOUR COMMUNICATION PERSONALITY TYPE

As you start to explore the different types, you may notice that you can fall into a different type for different areas of your life. You may have a tendency to be a particular "type" at work or with friends that is different from the type you are with your partner. The place to focus on for the purpose of this book is your relationship. What type do you default to when emotion gets triggered and you feel a conflict arising? Your communication personality type is:

- Determined by where you fall on the scale of *assertiveness* versus *flexibility.*
- Your personal tendencies for how you start conversations, react to what your partner says, respond to conflict, and process your emotions.
- Often your unconscious "comfort zone" for you and what you automatically default to without thinking (although human beings have the potential to evolve).

As a couple, you then have a communication dynamic, which is:

- The way your communication personality types interact with each other.
- A way for you to better understand each other and create harmony.

As you start to read about the different dynamics that can exist, you must know that there's no "right combination" or one that's better than another. Don't go thinking *maybe we're not a good fit because our dynamic is too different*. Every single dynamic has different angles, challenges, and benefits to it! You truly can find harmony with any combination if you learn to understand and leverage them.

Your communication personality types are based on two dimensions: assertive to reserved and flexible to inflexible. While you might assume you understand what each term means, let's make sure we're all on the same page. In their book *The Good Fight*[1] best-selling authors Drs. Les and Leslie Parrott use the terms expressiveness and flexibility to determine "The Four Fight Types" and how to express one's needs and meet the needs of a spouse. In our work with couples, we define them this way:

Assertive<—>Reserved: the degree to which you are open, comfortable, and proactive in expressing yourself, and what you want and need in the relationship. What does it mean to express yourself? Well first off, expressing yourself is not just talking. Some people would call themselves assertive because they talk a lot, but that's not what we mean by expressing yourself in the relationship. Expressing yourself must include: [clarity/detail] + [your authentic thought, feeling, idea, need, desire, emotion, or request].

Flexible<—>Inflexible: the degree to which you are willing and open to adjust your perspective, behaviors, and relationship roles based on changes to current circumstances and arising challenges. Being flexible isn't just saying "whatever you want" and letting your partner make all the decisions. You can be flexible, but then be resentful that your views aren't taken into account. Being flexible in this context is especially weighted on if you're open to shifting your

---

1   Parrott, Drs. Les and Leslie. *The Good Fight*. Tennessee: Worthy Publishing, 2013.

belief and perspective. Or at least, integrating your partner's perspective into yours to find a win-win solution. The flexibility dimension is important because there are seasons of a relationship in which different behaviors and roles will be called for.

As we go into explaining each "type" and the different dynamics, remember that this isn't about judging where your partner falls or wanting them to change; it's about understanding more about them and yourself. You will see each type broken down into bulleted traits. Even if you do not resonate with all of the bullet points listed, look for the two or three that describe you best to determine your type when triggered, or your default when conflict arises.

Type 1: Assertive/Inflexible (AI)

- You process through talking, but are less open to hearing your partner's viewpoint so you can often talk over them to dominate the conversation.
- You need a solution right away, and hate for emotional conversations to drag on.
- You can repeat yourself over and over if you are not feeling heard, and get more aggressive in your tone of voice if you don't get your way.
- You may need to have someone else in your life, outside of the circumstance, to talk with and help you calm down and see things differently.

Type 2: Assertive/Flexible (AF)

- You process through talking, and are more open to hearing your partner's perspective equally.
- You tend to commit to doing something, but then don't always follow through.
- You can initially be assertive when speaking your mind, but can often change it because you want to maintain peace in the relationship.

- You can easily bring up topics that are important to you, but then soon after forget about what was important to your partner, leading to recurring arguments.

Type 3: Reserved/Inflexible (RI)

- You process your thoughts and emotions silently on your own, but then you might not want to share your thoughts for fear of having to make a change or be disagreed with.
- If conflict arises, you may share your thoughts or feelings once, but then you'll shut down or retreat because you think you shouldn't have to repeat yourself.
- You can be silently frustrated and resentful when you don't get your way, but you keep it bottled up inside.
- You aren't proactive in sharing yourself, and can be resistant to when life circumstances need you to adapt.

Type 4: Reserved/Flexible (RF)

- You process your thoughts and emotions silently on your own, then you want to share and also hear your partner's perspective.
- If conflict arises, you can give "lip service" to try and move past or end it, but then not follow through on what you said.
- You can discount your own feelings, thinking they're not important and that you shouldn't bring them up to your partner.
- You are open to adapt as life circumstances change, but need your partner to make the decision and lead you into making that change.

Understanding your communication personality type can be one thing that is massively helpful for your self-awareness, but true harmony is achievable by understanding how your two types interact with each other aka your communication dynamic as a couple.

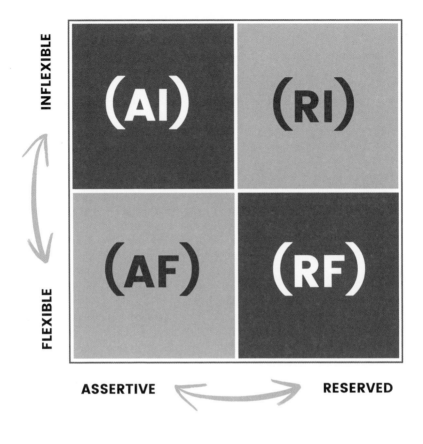

Before heading into this next section, do you know which type you most resonate with? Just to validate the accuracy of your initial guess, use the self-assessment questions below. You will also need to at least make the "assumption" of your partner's type, or better yet, have them go through the self-assessment as well.

SELF-ASSESS YOUR COMMUNICATION PERSONALITY TYPE

Score yourself for each question on a scale of 1–10:

Assertiveness

1. Open: how open am I in sharing all of my opinions, emotions, ideas, and needs with my partner?

A. 1: "I completely avoid opening up emotionally with my partner."

B. 5: "I am somewhat open, but feel apprehensive to share what feels like vulnerable opinions or needs."

C. 10: "I am 100 percent open with all things, I share the good and the bad."

D. My Score = _____ Partner's Score = _____

2. Comfortable: how comfortable am I in bringing up tough or vulnerable topics?

A. 1: "I completely avoid bringing up any challenging topics."

B. 5: "I will still bring up a challenging topic, but I have to do it at a particular time when the environment feels comfortable."

C. 10: "I feel no fear or discomfort in bringing up a challenging topic."

D. My Score = _____ Partner's Score = _____

3. Proactive: how proactive am I in bringing up topics before they become a bigger issue?

A. 1: "I am not proactive at all, and often wait till it already becomes a big problem and resentment is high."

B. 5: "I bring up important topics when I notice them, but it's usually once I'm more emotional already."

C. 10: "I bring up the topic the very second that I notice it so that it doesn't become something bigger."

D. My Score = _____ Partner's Score = _____

Assertiveness Scoring:

Add up all three scores for questions one, two, and three. Then, divide by three.

For example: #1 = 7 + #2 = 6 + #3 = 5 = (18)/3 = 6 (somewhat to moderately assertive)

My Total Score = _____ Partner's Total Score = _____

Interpreting your score:
- A score from 1–3 means you tend to be less assertive in your communication
- A score from 4–7 means you are somewhat to moderately assertive
- A score from 8–10 means you are very assertive in your communication

Now, score yourself for each of these questions on a scale of 1–10:

Flexibility

1. Willing to adjust your perspective: how willing am I to shift my perspective in respect to hearing my partner's perspective?
    A. 1: "I am not usually willing to shift my perspective, and I can be dismissive to my partner's perspective if I don't agree."
    B. 5: "I am sometimes open to shifting my perspective, but I have to be in the right mood."
    C. 10: "I am very open to hearing my partner's perspective, and will adjust my perspective with new information gathered."
    D. My Score = _____ Partner's Sore = _____
2. Willing to adjust behaviors: how willing am I to shift my behaviors based on changes in circumstances or arising challenges?
    A. 1: "I am not very willing to change my behaviors, and I resist it if my partner asks me to."

    B. 5: "I am somewhat willing to shift my behavior, but I might drag my feet on it until it's uncomfortable enough that I have to shift."

    C. 10: "I notice right away when a change in behavior is needed based on current circumstances, and I implement them right away."

    D. My Score = _____ Partner's Score = _____

3. Willing to adjust relationship roles: how open am I to changing my relationship roles based on current circumstances or arising challenges?

    A. 1: "I am not open to changing my relationship roles, and I just have to be accepted as I am."

    B. 5: "I am somewhat open to shifting my relationship roles, but I need to be told what's needed because I'm not good at identifying it myself."

    C. 10: "I can identify when a shift in relationship roles is needed for a season, and I make those changes right away."

    D. My Score = _____ Partner's Score = _____

Flexibility Scoring:

Add up all three scores for questions one, two, and three. Then, divide by three.

For example: #1 = 2 + #2 = 4 + #3 = 3 = (9)/3 = 3 (inflexible)

My Total Score = _____ Partner's Total Score = _____

Interpreting your score:

- A score from 1–3 means you tend to be more inflexible in your communication
- A score from 4–7 means you are somewhat to moderately flexible

- A score from 8–10 means you are very flexible in your communication

Using this self-assessment example, this person would be a 6 on the assertiveness scale, and a 3 on the flexibility scale. Using the 4 types, they would be the assertive/inflexible communication personality type (AI).

Bringing it all together:
Your Assertiveness Score = _____
Your Flexibility Score = _____
Your Communication Personality Type is _____
Your Partner's Assertiveness Score = _____
Your Partner's Flexibility Score = _____
Your Partner's Communication Personality Type is _____

THE MOST COMMON RELATIONSHIP DYNAMICS

Now that you have your self-assessment results, you must be excited to see how your "types" interact with each other! The interplay between your types is called your communication personality dynamic; and understanding your dynamic will help you identify recurring patterns and can give you a new perspective, clarity, and understanding on some of the things that felt previously frustrating about how you communicated with each other.

Dynamic 1: When both people are assertive/inflexible
One or both of you can feel any of the following:
- Like you have to "fight" for your opinion to be heard.
- That you both are quick (sometimes too quick) to share your opinion.
- That your dynamic feels very "fiery" at times.
- That seemingly simple conversations get escalated.
- That it's the other person that needs to change and not you.

YOUR COMMUNICATION PERSONALITY
DYNAMIC AS A COUPLE

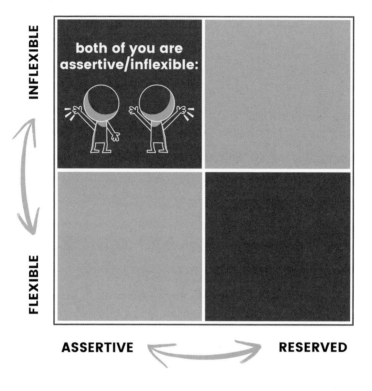

- If the topic is only important to one of you, you can be dismissive toward each other and your words can come off as "you're taking things too seriously."
- Your tone or attitude can sound like "this is what's happening" or "you need to listen to me" or "my way is best."

Now, we aren't just going to leave you hanging. In each of the dynamics we will also give you the tips, what we call "your personal work" to create more harmony in your communication dynamic together.

Your Personal Work:

- Reflect on how you can be more flexible (open to your partner's perspective).
- Try to ask your partner their opinion before you share yours.
- Be aware of which matters are really that important to you (versus which ones you are just arguing for).
- Realize that a decision doesn't need to be made right away.
- Focus on slowing down and writing down multiple resolutions together as a couple.

Dynamic 2: When both people are reserved/flexible

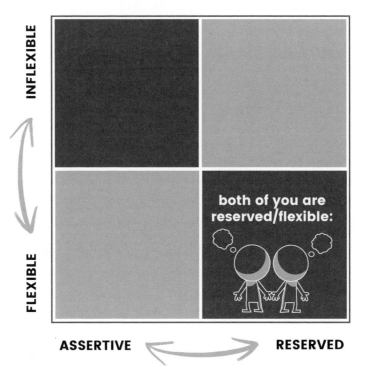

YOUR COMMUNICATION PERSONALITY DYNAMIC AS A COUPLE

INFLEXIBLE

FLEXIBLE

both of you are
reserved/flexible:

ASSERTIVE   RESERVED

One or both of you can feel any of the following:

- That you can "tolerate" a frustration for a while, but then get to a point where you blow up if resentment builds up.
- That you aren't quite sure if your partner really is okay/satisfied with something.
- You can assume they're happy because they didn't bring it up, but then find out that they would have preferred it go another way.
- That you have difficulty making important decisions together.

Your Personal Work:

- Don't assume that your partner is okay with something because they don't speak up. Ask more questions!
- Have regular check-in conversations to ensure you're both on the same page with the weekly family meeting guide (see on page 94).

Dynamic 3: When both are reserved/inflexible

One or both of you can feel any of the following:

- That you hold back your true feelings about a topic and then eventually let out your bottled-up frustration all at once.
- That you tend to retreat, shut down, and isolate when you're mad.
- You can be vague and unclear about what you desire, and get frustrated internally that your partner doesn't do something the way you wanted.

Your Personal Work:

- Set up a scheduled time each week to talk about any upsets you had that you didn't vocalize. Doing the family meeting will be very helpful for you. You may even find it helpful to

YOUR COMMUNICATION PERSONALITY DYNAMIC AS A COUPLE

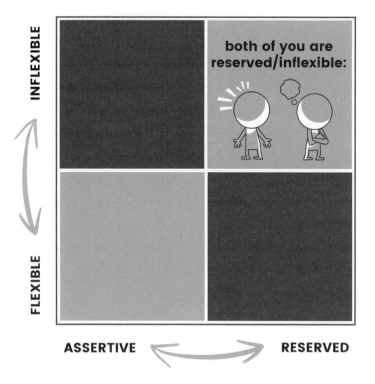

write down what you want to say ahead of time, rather than trying to gather your thoughts in the moment.

- Use active listening when your partner has their turn to share, and be more open to hearing out their perspective. When you are the speaker, say what your positive intent is for having this conversation. (For example: the intent is that we are more on the same page, and are able to understand each other more clearly.)

Dynamic 4: When one is assertive/inflexible and one is reserved/flexible

If you are the assertive/inflexible one, you can feel:

- Isolated when your partner is quiet.

YOUR COMMUNICATION PERSONALITY DYNAMIC AS A COUPLE

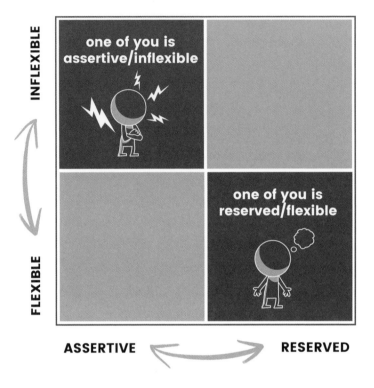

- Frustrated when you're making attempts to understand your partner but they don't share as openly as you do.
- You want to resolve conflicts right away, and you feel uncomfortable if something lingers.
- You process your emotions by talking, and can sometimes repeat yourself until you feel understood or get your way.

If you are the reserved/flexible one, you can feel:

- Dominated by your partner if they share their feelings in a way that seems overwhelming to you (tone of voice, speed, number of things said).
- Pressured to talk right away and before you're ready.

- You process your emotions quietly and often need time to think through them before you are ready to talk.

Your Personal Work:

For the assertive/inflexible one:

- Reflect on how you can be more open to hearing your partner's perspective and adapting to change and win-win solutions.
- Ask your partner their opinion before you share yours.
- Be aware of which matters are really important to you versus the ones you are just arguing for to be right.

For the reserved/flexible one:

- Share your preferences and don't just succumb to what your partner wants.
- Become more aware of the times you start to retract or revert to being passive in the conversation.
- Determine ways that make you feel more comfortable sharing (writing a note first, talking while on a walk, etc.).

Dynamic 5: When both are assertive/flexible

One or both of you can feel any of the following:

- That you both are able to share your perspectives, but have difficulty making decisions if you're overly flexible.
- That you can create plans but don't always follow through.
- That you start to talk over each other if you're triggered, and conversations might not get fully complete.

Your Personal Work:

- Sit down regularly and assess your priorities so you can reflect on and measure your progress.
- Make sure you both have emotional outlets besides each other so you maintain your individuality.

YOUR COMMUNICATION PERSONALITY DYNAMIC AS A COUPLE

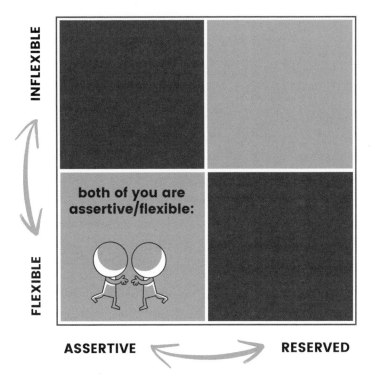

IMPROVING YOUR ASSERTIVENESS AND FLEXIBILITY

There are 10 total dynamics that you could fall into based on your individual types. We just wanted to cover the 5 most common ones we have found. The goal of understanding the assertiveness and flexibility scales isn't to try to change yourself or your partner, but one of the beautiful things about being human and also being open to self-development is that you can evolve and transform. Not when you're forced to by your partner, but when you're committed to it because you enjoy the growth journey. Do not feel like you are alone in this. Going back to the group of 78 diverse couples who took the relationship assessment, on a scale of 1–5 from very low to very high, the average level of assertiveness for partners was a

[2.87] which is on the border of low and average assertiveness in the relationship.

Being completely transparent, in prior relationships Jocelyn felt like she had to change herself to "fit" into what worked for her partner to try to keep the relationship going. She naturally has a more assertive personality type (and often inflexible), and that would often clash with her partners. At the time, her fear was that if she really expressed her authentic self, she would make her partners feel threatened and they would ultimately leave her. Her insecurities led to her molding herself to accommodate each relationship (like a chameleon), and that often meant diminishing her assertiveness to avoid conflict. She feared that she'd push away her partner if she shared her true opinions, feelings, or fear of being vulnerable.

In her upbringing Jocelyn saw women often submit to men and defer to their opinion. She saw women take the direction from men and hold back their perspective to avoid ruffling their feathers. While it wasn't spoken out loud, the buildup of these tiny memories created a belief that assertive women push men away. To make this belief system even more complex and confusing, she also saw these same women finally end up asserting themselves by exploding emotionally. Nope, not expressing . . . exploding. Since she didn't want to be the type of person that acted that way, she was often conflicted and unsure about how to assert herself in a healthy way. (Remember, there's no "Relationships 101" class in school.)

In romantic relationships, there would eventually come a point when she was either resentful, or had pent up thoughts and feelings to share, so she'd lash out and it would surprise her partner. She hadn't discovered a healthy in-between. So, when she started the relationship with me, her high level of assertiveness was very attractive, but she knew she had to unlearn her past tendencies to not fall into the same patterns of previous relationships. It was like a baby learning to walk—she'd take a few steps forward in progress, then overdo it, and fall down. So, when she started her own personal development journey, she wanted to discover what healthy assertiveness looks like and how to embody that. Not to change herself, but to reveal her most authentic self.

For you, your natural expression is different from others in your life and likely even from your partner, so the goal of this section isn't to alter what makes you powerful and unique, but instead to make you more adaptable in any conflict—allowing you to shorten the Argument Hangover period! Let's take a look at the definition of the Assertive<—>Reserved scale again: the degree to which you are open, comfortable, and proactive in expressing yourself. Being open will likely look different for you than for your partner. Being emotionally open is vulnerable, and, yes, it does take courage. If one of your primal fears is not being accepted and not belonging, here some questions you can reflect on:

- Am I willing to be more honest with myself about my true thoughts, feelings, and needs?
- Can I be more emotionally available to my partner by revealing vulnerable parts of myself?
- In what ways do I close myself off from sharing the things I fear my partner might judge or not understand?

One of the beautiful things about partnership is having someone to confide in and share the deeper parts of yourself. Take a risk, and explore how you can be even 5 percent more open with them. It's these types of conversations from the heart that connect you in more meaningful ways.

The second element of the Assertive<—>Reserved scale is being comfortable with sharing yourself with your partner. This is a great place for you to gain even more awareness about what you specifically need in order to feel safe sharing. For example, do you feel more at ease on a walk with your partner instead of sitting face to face at a table? Does it feel more natural writing it down in a letter before you have a conversation? Do you feel more open if music is playing? These are all different ways our more reserved clients have found to feel more comfortable to share themselves.

Here are a few questions to ponder on this topic:

- In what physical environment do I feel more comfortable opening up?
- What can I do differently in my current relationship to feel more comfortable (include more movement, sounds, etc.)?

The third element of the Assertive<—>Reserved scale is how proactive you are in sharing yourself with your partner. Being proactive is critical to healthy conflict in your partnership to avoid building up resentment that leads to escalated emotions. But again, your version of being proactive will likely be different from your partner. For them, it might mean bringing it up the very moment they notice something is off, and for you it might mean taking a couple of days to reflect on it, organize your thoughts, and then bring it up. Wherever you fall on the spectrum, the goal here is to be even a little more proactive than you are now. Could you bring up topics a little bit sooner? Could you open up even if you think it's something you can brush off your shoulders? Could you pause your busy to-do list to share what's on your mind first?

An excuse many couples have that blocks them from being proactive is that they are really busy and don't have the time. Please don't let your weekend errands and cleaning the house be more important than saying what you need to say. At the end of your life you won't think "gosh, I'm so happy we frantically crammed in our long to-do list each weekend." No, you'll either be grateful for how meaningful your connection was or regret the ordinary/routine way you approached your relationship. Your toilets can stay dirty for an extra hour! Your heart shouldn't have to withhold something that's important to you, or that will ultimately bring you more connection and understanding. What is your real priority? You may think it is your relationship, but the accurate way to see what you prioritize is to look at what you spend more of your time doing. You're neglecting yourself and hurting your relationship when you aren't proactive, all the while distracting yourself with completing menial tasks. Honestly, who cares about being busy? There is no prize (and certainly not a game we want to win) for who was the busiest couple! Rather than providing questions to reflect on for being proactive, we want to offer a few affirmations to practice:

- My thoughts and feelings are more important than my to-do list.
- I deserve to speak up and get things off my shoulders.
- It is toxic to hold things in and I commit to being 5 percent more proactive than I already am for the sake of our relationship.

Now that you've reflected on where you can expand your version of assertiveness, let's dive into how you can increase your level of flexibility. As a reminder, here is the definition of the Flexible<—> Inflexible scale: the degree to which you are willing and open to adjust your perspective, behaviors, and relationship roles based on changes to current circumstances and arising challenges. While some people assume the goal is to swing all the way to the left side of the dynamic to be completely flexible, you actually don't want to do that. It's possible to be overly flexible, just as much as it is to be overly inflexible. This is especially true if you're overly flexible year after year, because you can lose yourself in the relationship. This over-flexibility might be nice for two or three days for your partner on a vacation, but it can start to feel frustrating that you don't even recognize yourself over time. Your partner wants just that, a true active partner and not just a passive bystander to be in a relationship with. A partner is someone who contributes and challenges, not just succumbs or just says yes to everything they prefer. Since you probably read that and thought "I definitely don't want to lose myself in the relationship," let's dive into each element of this scale.

The first element of the Flexible<—>Inflexible scale is how willing you are to adjust your perspective. As human beings, this is a really challenging task. In your mind, you can be totally convinced that your view is the right one because you will find evidence of it! You may have heard the phrase "what you look for, you find." We are sure you have had the experience of buying a new car and thinking to yourself *I have not seen this style or color of this model on the road at all*. But what happens over the next week? You see no less than 10 other cars exactly like your new one! Is this because everyone just bought that same car this week? No. They were always there but you were not looking for them. So, just because you have a certain perspective does not mean it's universally true. You may have found evidence that it was true for you, but that's because you were out looking for it! This does not mean your partner's perspective is any less true than yours, because they have just as much proof that theirs is right, too!

When some people think of flexibility, they think of the cliché statement "a relationship requires compromise." But we aren't talking about compromise. Do you want a compromised arm or leg? Do you want the structure of a bridge you drive across to be compromised? Absolutely not! Compromise implies diminished strength and integrity, and not being whole. If you have gotten anything from this book it's that you want to strengthen your relationship, not weaken it. Compromising yourself only weakens your relationship as a whole. We never use the word compromise in our relationship because it can build up into resentment for having to give something up, or sacrifice what is important to you.

If you are unwilling to adjust your perspective, you are unfortunately addicted to being "right" and this will kill your relationship connection. Not only that, but you're likely missing out on discovering new and better things. Here are a few questions to ponder on this topic:

- Am I open to the possibility that maybe I am missing something in my perspective and I could be better served by trying to look from my partner's?
- Am I willing to let go of being "right" and more open to a new and better solution?
- What is even more beneficial about the way my partner sees the issue?

Let's go into the second element of the Flexibility<—>Inflexibility scale, which is how willing you are to adjust your behaviors. Look, we get it . . . you've been operating a certain way for years and it's comfortable. But maybe your actions aren't as beneficial as you think they are. Just check this out with us for a minute.

What we hear commonly from couples at our workshops is that their partner has been asking them to change some behavior, and they don't want to, like actions they take with money, their health, their children, or quality family time. For example, Rory and Brooklyn were perpetually getting into arguments about how they spent their evenings as a family after work. Brooklyn was frustrated every evening because they both would come home after a long day, and Rory would immediately go watch TV on the couch while she cooked. She would ask from the kitchen "so how was your day" and get a simple response like "it was okay but long." After a few attempts to connect without getting the attention back she hoped for, she would raise her voice and say "can you please just turn off the TV and help me cook and set up the table?" He'd respond poorly because he was tired and wanted to relax for a few minutes. But that often turned into a few hours at night of being silent on the couch. They both argued that the other person should be the one to change their actions. Rory thought that she should give him time to relax, and Brooklyn thought he should help her immediately with food and not watch TV as much. For months, they experienced disconnected evenings and their intimacy suffered for it. The way they both saw it, the other person should change their behavior.

Your version of this might be different. It might be about how the dishes are done, or how the children are disciplined, or how you each spend money. Regardless of the exact scenario you face, where are you unwilling to adjust your actions for the greater good of the relationship? That's what you have to realize. When you are unwilling to adjust them, even slightly, you are choosing to keep a recurring issue lingering on. And here's the sad truth: most of the time it's over really silly, ridiculous, menial things. We've watched couples end their marriages because they were unwilling to change one or two actions that really would not alter their individual lives that much yet would have made all the difference for the relationship to move forward.

It's important that we follow up that statement with also saying that we've seen many relationships also end because one or both people are overly flexible. Like we said earlier, if you just submit to everything your partner says and does because you fear conflict, you can lose sight of who you are. You've seen these real-life scenarios depicted in movies. One partner wakes up and goes "I haven't been seen or heard, I don't know who I am anymore and I want out." It's important for you to understand how flexible/inflexible you are in your relationship, so ponder on these questions:

- Has my partner been asking me to shift one of my actions that would be more beneficial to our relationship?
- Could I be even a little bit more willing to adjust my actions for us to have more harmony and love?
- Are there any places where I am overly flexible with my actions and have lost sight of myself?

Once you've explored those questions alone or together, let's move on to the third and final element of the Flexibility<—> Inflexibility scale: how willing you are to adjust your relationship roles. As we discussed earlier in the book, modern life demands you and your partner to play so many different roles. Within your relationship, you fit into certain relationship roles either by default or by choice. Falling into your relationship roles by default means you just adopted them because that's what you learned growing up, or society modeled them for you. For example, "the woman always cooks" or "the husband handles money." Those gender-based roles are becoming more and more outdated. Two reasons why those default designations don't work are:

1. It's not based on who is more skilled at that role.
2. Different seasons of the relationship require different roles.

Unfortunately, if you're not willing to be somewhat flexible with relationship roles, you'll experience massive tension when challenges arise. That's why the latter part of the Flexibility<—>Inflexibility scale says "based on changes to current circumstances and arising challenges," because your circumstances will change, you will encounter life challenges, and you don't want to be plagued by inner resentment that your role might have to be adjusted for a season.

One couple shared at our couples workshop that they were arguing a lot because the previous year she had experienced a traumatic car accident and was not able to work more than a few hours per week. Not only that, but she was also limited in her ability to help around the house and with the kids. He was withdrawing emotionally from the relationship because he resented that he had to take on relationship roles that he didn't expect to. He was so used to their dynamic of him going to work, coming home to dinner prepared, and a clean home that he resisted the change. Of course, he felt terrible for his wife's injury, but he was not adapting emotionally to the change. It was to the point where they were actually considering divorce.

Before you jump to potentially judging him and thinking "oh my gosh, he shouldn't be so upset that she was injured," this is more common than you might think even outside of injuries. For example, one partner doesn't want to admit that the other is better with money because they "should" be the one that manages it. From an emotional perspective, what if your partner is having a few rough months and needs you to step up and lead. Do you rise to the challenge?

Just because your relationship started one way, doesn't mean it will always be that way, especially when it comes to your relationship roles. Maybe there's an even better way for you two to operate as a team—whether for a season or for years.

Here are a few questions to reflect on this:

- If we set aside all gender-based roles that we've been taught, who is actually better at some of the main roles in our family? (For example: finances, discipline, cooking, etc.)
- Based on the season we're in, could I evolve my relationship roles to be even more supportive to the type of relationship and life we both want?

In closing out this section, remember that the goal of understanding the assertiveness and flexibility scales isn't to try and change yourself or your partner. It's about self-awareness on a moment by moment basis. As a human being, you aren't stuck a certain way and you can evolve (and are actually supposed to)! Every moment in your relationship is brand new and might call upon you to adapt in some way. Your expression of these two scales might be different, but it's about showing your partner that you're willing to evolve when it benefits the relationship. As you two integrate the words assertiveness and flexibility into your relationship vocabulary together, you can lovingly remind each other if one of you has gone too far on the spectrum. (The key word being lovingly.)

YOUR GAME PLAN

- Determine your communication personality type, your partner's type, and your dynamic.
- Remember it's not about changing the way your partner communicates, but understanding their communication personality type.
- Identify moments when your communication dynamics are creating tension.
- Understand the elements of assertiveness and flexibility, and focus on being aware of where you fall on those scales on a moment by moment basis. Then you can adapt to better serve your relationship in that season.

You can shorten the Argument Hangover by understanding and leveraging your communication personality types.

9

THE INGREDIENTS FOR LOVE

"Love is a true thing if it is made up of a substance called understanding."
—Thich Nhat Hanh (nominated for the Nobel Peace Prize by Martin Luther King Jr.)

The point of this entire book has been to help you shorten the Argument Hangover period (recover from it faster), and empower you to fight smarter as a couple. By incorporating the tools throughout, you will increase your ability to stay in a place of connection and love with your partner and stay on the same team, no matter what challenges arise. You now have the opportunity to see conflict as something that strengthens your relationship, and doesn't have to be something you avoid!

But perhaps you have noticed one missing requirement for a great relationship that we have not mentioned yet. That is *love*! It's true we have not yet talked much about love up till this point, and you could also say that this is what all of this has been leading to. We held off talking about it until now because the word "love" has been used so many times in many different ways, that you may not even clear about what love really means.

If we asked you what true love really is, what would you say? If we wrote down all the answers right here that couples from our workshops have said, or what your parents told you, what you have seen in movies, or even where you have experienced the sensation of love through-out your relationship or life, it would take up the next few pages. You would see a wide range of many different answers. Doesn't the fact that there are so many different answers show that you don't *really* know, and neither do very many other people? Love by default can be:

- A feeling in your body
- The coming and going of emotion
- When you feel trust and security
- Enough shared experience and compatibility
- Having a companion so you are not alone
- The actions and things your partner does for you
- Something you have to say because you are "blood" family
- Something you can fall "in" and "out" of

Are these answers what true love is? Think back on when you first said "I love you" to your partner. Didn't it feel amazing the moment you declared that to each other? You might even smile as you reminisce about that powerful moment. But what about now? How do you know that love is still there, or that it will be strong and alive in the future? Especially when years have passed or you've gone through tough times.

Is love really a "fleeting feeling" that can come and go based on conditions in your relationship? It unfortunately is for many couples. But that's *not* true love! Love is one of the most mysterious and dif-ficult to describe human experiences. There's not an exact way to "measure" its existence. It's not like measuring flour for a cake recipe. So, without a clear way to determine what true love is, how do you actually keep it there? The simple answer is that you are just guess-ing or assuming it will just be there. Being completely honest here, assuming something will just be there is a way to ensure it will not.

Yet do not despair, that's exactly why you are reading this book and specifically what this chapter is going to allow you to do! When you get clear on the elements that allow love to be present and experienced, you will have a way of knowing and measuring when it is in your relationship and when it is not. When it is not, you will know what to do to bring yourself back into its experience because love doesn't actually "go anywhere."

THE FOUR ELEMENTS OF LOVE

For this topic, we are going to refer to someone that gave their entire life to uncovering the process of experiencing peace and love, and then helping others do the same. For this, Thich Nhat Hanh was even nominated for the Nobel Peace Prize by Martin Luther King Jr. The opening quote for this chapter said "Love is a true thing if it is made up of a substance called understanding." Here are four elements of love[1] that you can use to measure whether you are living in a way with your partner for true love to be expressed and experienced:

> **Kindness:** Having the desire to bring happiness to your part-
> ner and actually having the ability to do so. Just having the
> desire to bring happiness to your partner is not enough if
> you do not have the ability to do so. You must take the right
> actions for both of you to experience happiness. This means
> that you cannot always be focused on yourself! When you
> have been together for a number of years, your attention can
> easily go to your other roles (like parenting, work, or even
> things like your phone). When this happens, there's less atten-
> tion to learning more about them, understanding them, and
> supporting them in their own individual growth. Kindness,
> to us, has a sense of slowing down in life, not having your
> attention dissipated in so many areas, so you can focus on
> what is most important in your life. It's having grace for your
> partner, a continued interest in them as an individual, and an

---

1   Hanh, Thich Nhat. *True Love: A Practice for Awakening the Heart.* Boulder: Shambhala Publications Inc., 1997.

attitude that is open, ready to forgive, and let things go when conflicts arise within your partnership.

- **Compassion:** Having the desire to ease the pain or suffering of your partner and actually having the ability to do so. Did you forget that your partner actually feels sadness, pain, or even suffering at times? It may not be from you, but from life circumstances that come up for them individually. Oh, yeah, guess what? Your partner is still actually having their own individual human experience. They may feel sad, hurt, or disappointed at times. Do you have compassion for them in these moments, even if it doesn't make sense to you? Even if you do not see a situation the same, do you still want to help them get back to a place of peace, certainty, and trust that it's all going to work out? Do you know the actions to take (have you actually asked them) that will effectively help and support them? Compassion is expressed through having empathy for whatever your partner is going through and not trying to just fix them or get them to move passed situations when they feel emotion.

- **Joy:** The anticipation of good. Joy is different from happiness because it is not based on current circumstances, and is not just a mood. Joy comes from creating a compelling future for your life together and progressing toward it. You have the desire to bring joy to your partner and have the ability to do so. You can spend all day thinking or talking about how you want your life to be. But is that the life your partner also wants? Have you sat down to ask what would bring your partner joy? Even if at one time you were aligned and on the same page, things and people change, do they not? Are your current actions aligned for the vision and goals you both have together? If so, it is a joy to be realizing that vision as a couple. Earl Nightingale said "success is the progressive realization of a worthy ideal." What a joy it is to do that as a couple. If you are not feeling joy, refer back to the weekly family meeting on page 94 to get clarity and set aligned goals for your relationship.

- **Freedom:** In true love you actually attain freedom, both of you. When you love someone, they should feel freer and not constrained. Does your partner feel free inside and out? Do they feel they can pursue what calls to them and what brings joy into their own life? Do they feel freedom to open up to you about things in life (and about your relationship) that they are not thrilled about? Do they feel they can tell you about the things that make them sad or have brought pain or suffering into their life experience? If your partner feels suppressed, meaning they have to hold things back to not rock the boat, make you mad, or cause a conflict, this is the opposite of freedom. By being in a relationship with you, your partner should feel more freedom to be who they desire to be.

> A partnership where both people feel complete freedom to be themselves and thrive is a truly empowered couple!

These are the four elements of true love. After reading these four elements you may feel empowered to have more conversations with your partner, or you may be inspired by some new actions! This is how you can truly create something new. However, you may also be in the place where it just became strikingly obvious that certain elements are missing in your relationship. But the only way to improve is to have awareness of where you are now, and then take new actions.

You likely noticed a common thread within each of the four elements of love. Your desire for kindness, compassion, joy, and freedom is just not enough. It is of course what is first needed, but you must develop the ability to keep these elements present. Imagine you wanted to be a professional athlete, famous chef, or actor. Is that desire in itself enough for you to become those things? Once again, no. There are many other people that desire for that dream as well. But such a small percentage of people have realized that dream. So, what was the difference? It was that those people discovered what it would take, and then consistently learned the skills to develop the ability to become great at what they do. In the same manner, you must develop your own abilities for each of the four elements of love so that kindness, compassion, joy, and freedom are all experienced within the relationship.

SUCCESS IS PROGRESS AND PROGRESS IS HAPPINESS

It should not feel like a burden to develop the necessary skills for the sake of consistently having love present and alive in your relationship. It can actually be an enjoyable, empowering experience! What better pursuit can there be than to practice and live the four elements of love? (With the key word being practice!)

An encouraging statement was made by Tony Robbins when he said "progress equals happiness." It doesn't say "perfection equals happiness."[2] It's about moving forward, and being better than you were yesterday. You will not be perfect with everything you learned in this book, and neither will your partner. That's okay, be quick to forgive if you fall into old patterns for a moment. You can't just read this book once and expect to fight smarter, communicate better, and shorten your Argument Hangovers. The fact is this book gives you knowledge and skills, but the real difference comes from putting those into action. Knowledge in action is wisdom! So, we encourage

---

2   Robbins, Tony. 2017. "Tony Robbins: This is the secret to happiness in one word." CNBC. https://www.cnbc.com/2017/10/06/tony-robbins-this-is-the -secret-to-happiness-in-one-word.html.

you to keep this book somewhere visible that you can pick up and review as you take action in your day to day life with your partner.

You and your partner can be each other's biggest support system and cheerleaders as you make progress in your relationship. Say something out loud when you notice they implemented a new skill from the book, like "hey, I noticed you were much calmer in our last disagreement, and you really kept to the agreements we made, that was great!" Or "I really appreciated how you listened to me when I shared my feelings last night. I felt really understood." Every single positive statement adds up. We can be so quick to give "negative" feedback to our partner, and neglect to acknowledge the positive changes and actions taken. We will give you two simple things that will keep you progressing forward as a team no matter what season you are in: gratitude and attention.

Gratitude has been one of the most powerful gifts for our relationship. For us, gratitude is a chosen perspective. You might not wake up every day feeling extremely grateful, because you're human. Gratitude really is a consistent and intentional practice. We all know the saying "you can see the half glass full or half empty," when it comes to life in general, but that often doesn't get applied to romantic relationships. We know you love and appreciate your partner, but do you make it known to them? We encourage you to say out loud all of the things you are grateful for about them. Yes, even if you had a disagreement last night or even if you are annoyed with something they did recently! It's easy to be grateful when everything is going your way and feels good in life. But imagine being grateful for even the challenging moments or lessons in your relationship. Write down, or better yet, tell your partner five things you're grateful for right now. Here are some examples:

- I am so grateful that you have chosen to be my partner
- I am so grateful that I wake up next to you in the morning

- I am so grateful that you get me a cup of coffee in the morning
- I am so grateful for how hard you work for our family
- I am so grateful that you read this book with me
- I am so grateful that you aim to grow with me

Whether you feel extremely happy in your current season of relationship, or you're going through a tough time, you can always benefit from focusing on what you can be grateful for. There is always something, even if it's to be alive! No one ever said "I'm all capped out on gratitude, I don't need anymore." So, consider this a friendly reminder to cultivate an attitude of gratitude. For all of the fun, beautiful moments you have together, but also for the challenges you've overcome together.

Earlier we gave you the skills to be able to actually listen to your partner, and you just got the four elements of true love. Neither of these could happen without you first giving your undivided attention. Here is the proof. Why is it that young kids will interrupt your conversations with another adult or your partner? Why when you are on the phone, watching a movie, or reading a book will a kid jump in front of you, wave their hands, say your name over and over, or even try to show you a painting they just made while you are walking out the door for work? They are trying to get your attention! Because without having to think about it they know if they get your attention, they are a priority, they are important to you, and that you love them.

This honestly is so important because your attention is the only thing you actually have to give in this world! Everything you think you can give to your partner (your time, energy, heart, soul, life), can only be given once you have first given your attention. This is the only real thing you have to give and is the only real way to give love to your partner! Though that is a powerful statement about giving your attention, it actually is one of the easiest things to do.

Sometimes we all just forget to do it. Here is the shortest exercise you will ever do but one that will have the biggest impact on being able to always make progress in your relationship.

Giving Your Full Attention Exercise:
1. With no distractions, sit directly facing your partner so that your knees, shoulders, heart, and head are all directly in front of them.
2. Without talking or making any faces or gestures to each other, look directly into each other's eyes.
3. For just one minute, continue to just look into their eyes without initially laughing, smirking, or even smiling.

At first you may feel weird, uncomfortable, or silly not to smile or make a face. But notice how all of that is your own resistance to just completely giving your undivided attention to your partner. If this is something you feel resistance to, it may be a reflection of how little undivided attention you actually give your partner. But stay with the exercise for the full minute, and by the end you are free to express whatever you want. At that point you can laugh, cry, hug, kiss, or even be intimate! (As a side note, this exercise is actually a great way to enter into physical intimacy with your partner.) Many couples that do this one-minute exercise shockingly say "I feel more seen and understood than I have in years!" Without doing the exercise you might think "how can you feel understood without saying anything?" The answer of course is attention. Attention is the key to understanding and the pathway to love.

Before closing out this chapter on love, we would regret not at least mentioning the difference between what we call "fantasy love" and "healthy love." Too many people live with misguided ideas of what maintaining love really takes for a long-lasting relationship. We call it a "fantasy" because it's built on unrealistic expectations and conditions, not personal responsibility and choice.

> Your partner cannot make you happy, you make yourself happy.

You can't wait for your partner to do things that deserve your love. You must act from *being loving* first. You can't expect the reasons you fell in love to be what keeps you in love. Werner Erhard said one of the most profound things about love, summarized as "love is a declaration." Love doesn't last if it's a conditional mood or feeling. Do you see love as a verb or a noun? Do you say "I love you" as a reaction or a decision? We invite you to see love as something you choose unconditionally, which drives you to take loving actions that nurture the feelings of love within your relationship.

FANTASY LOVE **VS** HEALTHY LOVE

- you make me happy
- I shouldn't "rock the boat" & create conflict
- you will anticipate my needs
- our love is all we need, and it will never change

- I'm responsible for my happiness
- we can disagree in healthy ways
- I must share my needs openly
- we must learn ways to keep our love alive

YOUR GAME PLAN

We discovered a lot together in this book, so let's do a brief recap. First, you gained a new term for the period of time after you have a disagreement that lasts until you resolve it emotionally and reconnect, which is the Argument Hangover. You can use that phrase in funny ways together like "hey, our Argument Hangover was only thirty minutes this time! We're making progress!" We hope that this new terminology helps it feel less personal to you and your relationship.

Next, you uncovered some of the outdated and destructive beliefs that can have you resist and avoid conflict. You can now see conflict as an opportunity to clarify what you do want, and a way to become even more connected to each other. Remember that both of your perspectives are valid, and there doesn't have to be one "winner" and one "loser" in a disagreement.

You went through the three aspects of your emotional triggers: the triggering event, the triggered feeling, and the triggered action. You'll always be human, but you can now take responsibility and have awareness of when you're triggered and choose a different action. Ultimately, by honoring your agreements for times of conflict, your triggered actions won't cause as much damage during a conflict.

Then you journeyed on to the tools you can implement before, during, and after conflict. We talked about the importance of making frequent deposits to your partner's love account, and telling your partner if yours is low. You can eliminate many of your conflicts by implementing the weekly family meeting because it's where you'll catch anything important before it builds into resentment.

For the times you are in a disagreement, you can focus on actually listening to your partner so they feel understood, even if you don't agree. You have prompts for using we-based language instead of you-based language, which lends to staying on the same team and solving the problem together. Plus, you now understand the importance of being clearer with your communication so that your partner isn't left in the dark as to what you need and desire.

To ensure your conflicts are fully resolved and that you aren't tolerating a subtle Argument Hangover, you can implement the 5 R's: reflect, responsibility, remind, reconnect, and reconcile. Remember that getting busy and just brushing things under the rug doesn't mean it's fully resolved.

Next you identified your communication personality type, and what your dynamic is as a couple. The goal is not to change your partner or resist their communication style, but for both of you to be able to adapt your level of assertiveness and flexibility for what your relationship needs in each season.

And last but not least, we talked about the four elements of true love and setting your sights on progress, not perfection, in your relationship. When you maintain an attitude of gratitude, and give sufficient attention to your partner/relationship, you are a truly empowered couple that can handle any challenge that comes your way!

Please stay in touch with us: connect with us on social media, online on our website, or even at one of our in-person or online workshops. As we type this last section here, we are imagining you reading this book. In fact, we're writing this very sentence in the middle of the COVID-19 pandemic when we've realized more than ever that human relationships are critical to feeling happiness. It truly matters to us that we get to know you and can support you on your journey to being an empowered couple!

—In gratitude, Aaron and Jocelyn, "The Freemans"

INDEX